First published in 2007
by Faber and Faber Limited
3 Queen Square London WC1N 3AU

Printed in the United Kingdom by Butler and Tanner

A CIP record for this book
is available from the British Library

ISBN 978–0–571–23779–1

2 4 6 8 10 9 7 5 3 1

This book
belongs to:

........................................

# THE QI ANNUAL

## 'E'

### edit

Edited by John Lloyd

Art Direction by David Costa

ff

*faber and faber*

# Stephen here!

Ee, ye be reet well and cheerly greeted, deer reeder t't letter E. The clever elves tell me, the endless need...

No, no, no. This just isn't going to work. I had planned to write an introduction containing only our hero letter, 'E', but aside from the level of difficulty, I suddenly realised, with a stab of wonder and joy, that I couldn't be sedding, beggering ersed.

For a nation, many of whom who grew up on the *Blue Peter Annual*, the arrival of the *QI Annual* must surely be a cause of nothing but rapture and enchantment of the highest, giddiest kind. If we are to enter a new Age of Annuals then perhaps all is not quite lost with our vulgar, etiolated and degraded culture? V-necked and sandalled, lying on our tummies, felt-pens or wax crayons at the ready, we leaf through the big pages not daring to take everything in at once, for the pleasures and secret corners of each page must be saved to the end like the fruity veins of a raspberry ripple. Hurrah for annuals, hurrah for puzzles and facts and drawings. Hurrah for... oh Lord, I think I've polluted myself.

Look, the point is that this is sent to you in love and friendship from all at QI, who have no higher aim, and no lower, than to please.

QI – changing the world one letter at a time.

*Stephen Fry*

# A message from the Editor

*Hi there Fact Nuts,*

*Welcome to the QI 'E' Annual!*

*We think this one is even better than the 'A', 'B', 'C' and 'D' Annuals. You may have missed those. We certainly did.*

*Most people felt they were a bit on the 'blank' side – or 'non-existent', as one bookworm put it.*

*Hopefully, we have put all that to rights in this super E edition. It's packed with E-type information – plus, there are cartoons, games and quizzes; loads of articles by your favourite QI celebs; and a chance to win £1,000 in cash!*

*We hope this will be the first of many QI Annuals, so please write to us and tell us what you think – what you liked and what you didn't like – so that we can make it even better next year. And let us know which letter is your favourite: 'R' perhaps, or maybe 'Y'.*

*Mr Fry's QI Elves are online round-the-clock, slaving away in the QI nugget mines on your behalf. Drop in for a chinwag at www.qi.com/E*

*See you there! Your chum,*

*'JumpingJack' Lloyd*

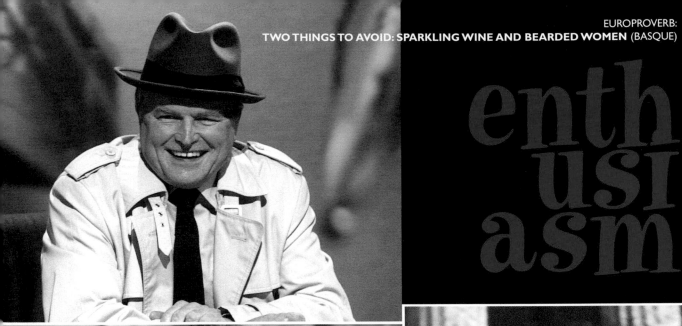

enth
usi
asm

Eric comes from the Old Norse name *Eirikr*, meaning 'ever ruler'. Notorious Viking **ERIC BLOODAXE** was the son of the far more genteel sounding King Harold Finehair of Norway. Bloodaxe was referred to in one Latin text as *Fratris Interfector*, or 'brother killer'. He is thought to have earned his gory nickname not through the everyday axework associated with rape and pillage, but rather by having craftily murdered anything up to nineteen of his own blood brothers in order to guarantee his succession to the throne.

The world's wealthiest Eric is **ERIC SCHMIDT**, chairman and CEO of Google Inc. In 2007 'Forbes' magazine ranked him the 116th richest man in the world, with an estimated $6.2 billion. He is also a director of Apple Inc.

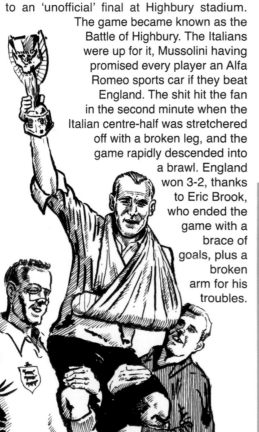

The 1930s truly were the 'golden age' of Erics in English football. Only four Erics have ever worn the famous Three Lions jersey, and three of them did so during that decade. One was **ERIC BROOK** of Manchester City, whose goals helped England win the 1934 World Cup. Having declined an invitation to compete in that year's competition (on the grounds that they would win it too easily) the English FA then challenged the eventual winners, Italy, to an 'unofficial' final at Highbury stadium. The game became known as the Battle of Highbury. The Italians were up for it, Mussolini having promised every player an Alfa Romeo sports car if they beat England. The shit hit the fan in the second minute when the Italian centre-half was stretchered off with a broken leg, and the game rapidly descended into a brawl. England won 3-2, thanks to Eric Brook, who ended the game with a brace of goals, plus a broken arm for his troubles.

Another Viking, **ERIC THE RED,** took his name from his ginger hair, and not from the mists that often enveloped him. His boisterous behaviour saw him evicted first from Norway, then from Iceland. Ironically, Eric the Red is credited with discovering Greenland, which he named after the colour of the vegetation thereon, as opposed to the colour of his beard. Eric the Red was the father of Leifr Eiriksson, the first European to have landed in North America (as opposed to Leif Erickson the American actor who played Big John Cannon in the popular 1960s televison series *The High Chaparral*).

# ERICS
## *through the ages*

Throughout history people called Eric have played a major role in shaping the world in which we live. Here is just a small selection of exceptional yet often unsung Erics.

English sculptor **ERIC GILL** created the iconic Gill Sans typeface in 1928. For many years it was the standard type used on all Penguin book jackets, as well as on railway signs and posters. Gill also designed postage stamps for the Royal Coronation in 1937. His erotic engraving 'Eve', featuring a naked bird and a snake, is regarded by many as his most important work. Gill was obsessed with the erotic, often requiring life models to perform sex while he sculpted. He was also a big fan of cocks. One of his lesser known works, 'Studies of Parts', is a sketch book containing dozens of detailed drawings of male members belonging to himself and his friends. For all his artistic ability, Gill appears to have been, even by modern-day standards, a raving pervert. His diaries reveal that he had regular sex with his sister Gladys, he sodomised his daughters, and according to his own notes, on December 8th 1929 he successfully concluded a sexual experiment with his dog.

Former Royal Navy officer Captain **ERIC 'WINKLE' BROWN, CBE, DSC, AFC, FRAeS, RN** has flown more types of aircraft than anyone else in history - 487 to be precise (and that's not including variants, such as the many different models of Spitfire he has flown). He is also the Fleet Air Arm's most decorated pilot. Brown was a test pilot whose job involved evaluating captured enemy aircraft following the Second World War. In December 1945 he became the first pilot to land a jet aircraft on a carrier when he brought a de Havilland Sea Vampire down onto the deck of HMS *Ocean*. This was one of 2,407 carrier landings in his career. Another world record. Well done Eric!

Bingo boss **ERIC MORLEY** was the man who put the glitterballs into British TV. The Dunkirk veteran kicked-off his kitsch campaign in 1949 when he launched *Come Dancing*, and two years later he brought the infamous Miss World TV beauty pageant into our living rooms. Morley also stood as Tory candidate for Dulwich in the 1979 general election. When the results were announced (in reverse order of course), Eric had lost by a mere 122 votes. That was one rare occasion when Morley declined to kiss the winner.

Thanks to spray paint, colourfully applying your name to the side of a train or a subway wall only takes seconds. But if it wasn't for Norwegian **ERIC ROTHEIM** young graffiti artists would be labouring away for hours with tins of paint and a brush. Scientist Eric patented his design for the first aerosol spray can in 1928. And in 1998, Norway, a nation not over-burdened with national heroes, issued a special postage stamp to celebrate their ingenious Eric's achievement.

The man responsible for Big Brother was an Eric. In George Orwell's novel, Big Brother was the dictator of a totalitarian state in which the entire population was under constant surveillance. The book's title was to have been *1980*, and then *1982*, but its publication was delayed due to Orwell's poor health. When it was eventually published in 1949 it was called *1984*. Orwell was not the author's original name either. It was the pen name chosen by **ERIC ARTHUR BLAIR**. Eric chose his new moniker from a shortlist of four, the runners-up being being Kenneth Miles, H. Lewis Allways and P.S. Burton. Orwell died from tuberculosis in January 1949, shortly after the book was published. And so, mercifully, he never got to see the television series his classic work inspired.

His moustache may not be familiar to you, but actor **ERIC THOMPSON**'s voice would be. When asked to narrate an English translation of the French TV series *Le Manège Enchanté*, Eric ignored the original scripts. Instead he watched the French programmes without the soundtrack, then made up his own stories to match the action. Thus *The Magic Roundabout* was born. A *Playschool* presenter in the 1960s, Eric was an accomplished thespian but seldom performed on TV. One of his rare television drama appearances came in 1966 when he played a Huguenot in a Dalek-free episode of *Dr Who* set in 16th-century Paris. Sadly Eric died in 1982. Actresses Emma and Sophie Thompson are his daughters.

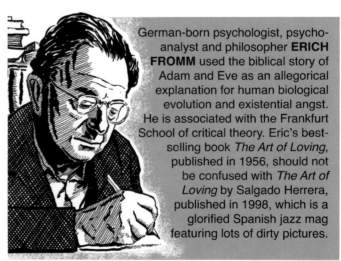

German-born psychologist, psycho-analyst and philosopher **ERICH FROMM** used the biblical story of Adam and Eve as an allegorical explanation for human biological evolution and existential angst. He is associated with the Frankfurt School of critical theory. Eric's best-selling book *The Art of Loving*, published in 1956, should not be confused with *The Art of Loving* by Salgado Herrera, published in 1998, which is a glorified Spanish jazz mag featuring lots of dirty pictures.

# EIGHT

There are eight protons in an oxygen atom; eight pinches in
a teaspoon; eight quavers in a note; and eighty-eight notes on a piano.
Wagner said that the first eight notes of 'Rule Britannia' summed up the whole of
the British character. Eight days is the amount of time needed to get used to glasses that
turn the images on your retina upside down. When you take them off, it takes less than eight
hours for everything to return to normal. The Irish playwright Brendan Behan became an alcoholic at
the age of eight. On her eighth birthday, Shirley Temple got 135,000 birthday presents. Eight was the
average age for choirboys to be castrated in 17th-century Italy. Unsupported breasts move in a figure-of-
eight motion when running. Both male and female ferrets have eight nipples. Quolls are carnivorous marsupials
native to Australia and Papua New Guinea that copulate continuously for eight hours. The first of the world's first
surviving octuplets was born in Houston, Texas, on December 8th, 1998. The rest were born by Caesarean section
on December 20th. The amount of cloud in the sky is measured in oktas. Eight oktas means the sky is totally
overcast. In 2001, the Ministry of Defence spent £260 million on eight Chinook helicopters. They couldn't be flown
because the MOD didn't have the software codes, and the US wouldn't release them for security purposes. The
House of Commons Public Accounts Committee described the purchase as 'one of the worst acquisitions' it had
ever seen. Cows are descended from extinct wild oxen called aurochs, a word that is both singular and plural.
An aurochs bull stood eight feet tall. In *The Gallic Wars*, Julius Caesar described it as only slightly smaller
than an elephant. The last recorded aurochs was killed in a Polish forest in 1627. The Spanish dollar or
peso was common currency in the US well into the 19th century. It was often cut into eight pieces
for small change – hence the term 'pieces of eight'. Two-eighths make a quarter, so a quarter
dollar (25 cents) is known as 'two bits'. There are eight bits in a byte; eight furlongs in a
mile; eight tablespoons in a gill and eight fluid ounces in a cup. There are eight
Lords a-leaping. Coca-Cola was invented in 1888. In the first eight
months of his new business, John Stith Pemberton
managed to sell less than half a dozen drinks a
day, despite the fact that he claimed it would cure morphine
addiction, indigestion, headache, neurasthenia and impotence. On his death
in Atlanta, Georgia, later the same year, no Coca-Cola at all was sold throughout the
city as a mark of respect. According to the Harvard Education School, there are eight kinds of
intelligence: Linguistic, Logical, Musical, Bodily, Spatial, Interpersonal, Intrapersonal and Naturalist.
Charles Darwin spent eight years studying barnacles before he wrote *The Origin of the Species*. The poet
Samuel Taylor Coleridge went for eight years without seeing his children. The philosopher Kierkegaard studied
theology at university for eight years without ever taking an exam. In 1890, Frenchman Clément Ader achieved the first
powered take-off in a steam-powered aircraft. It reached an altitude of eight inches. Italian anatomist Gabriello Fallopio,
after whom Fallopian tubes are named, designed a condom made from linen that was tied on with a pink ribbon. It was eight
inches long. Leeches and Hercules beetles can both grow to eight inches long. Mammoths' penises were eight inches in
diameter. The Republic of Maldives is in the *Guinness Book of Records* as The World's Flattest Country. There are more than a
thousand islands in the Republic, 80% of which are less than a metre above sea level and none of which attains a height of more
than eight feet. Eight is a lucky number in Japanese. Toyota is named after the company's founder, Sakichi Toyoda, who changed
his name to Toyota because in Japanese it is written in eight characters. The first box of Crayola (sold for 5 cents in 1903) had
the same eight colours found in the box today: red, blue, yellow, green, violet, orange, black and brown. The 1960s cartoon
superhero 'The Eighth Man' increased his strength by smoking cigarettes. The average Greek smokes eight cigarettes a day.
Octopus is Greek for eight feet. The giant Brazilian otter can be eight feet long. Britons use eight billion plastic bags a year.
In the 11th century there were eight vineyards in Essex. Sweden was a good place to be eight in 1994. At the beginning
of the year, there were 112,521 eight-year-old girls; by the end of the year, every single one of them was still alive.
Eight US publishers rejected George Orwell's *Animal Farm*. One of them kindly explained: 'We are not doing
animal books this year.' According to the World Conservation Union, one in eight bird species is at risk of
extinction. The last execution in the Tower of London took place on Thursday, August 14th, 1941,
when Josef Jakobs, a German spy, was shot by an eight-man firing squad. Subatomic
particles are classified by means of the Eightfold Way. The way to enlightenment is
via the eight steps of Buddhism's Noble Eightfold Path. An eight on its
side represents infinity and there are
**888 words on this page.**

# NINE 'E' THINGS THAT COME IN BATCHES OF NINE

**1. EXTRA TERRESTRIALS** *The first flying saucers were a group of nine unidentified objects spotted by travelling salesman Kenneth Arnold from his private plane on June 24th, 1947. He described them as moving at 1,200 mph like 'pie plates skipping over the water'. A newspaper coined the phrase 'flying saucer' and within weeks there were hundreds of such sightings. The likeliest explanation is that they were a mirage, the reflection of the nine snow-capped peaks of the Cascade Mountains in Washington, some sixty miles away.* **2. ELMS** Nine Elms in Vauxhall, London, is home to New Covent Garden Market, the capital's wholesale fruit and veg hub, relocated in 1974 from Covent Garden, where it had stood for more than 400 years. Battersea Power Station and Battersea Dogs Home are also in Nine Elms. To be 'battersea'd' was 18th-century slang for being treated for venereal disease. Herbs used to cure the condition were sold in Battersea Market. **3. ELLICE ISLANDS** *The South Pacific island group formerly known as the Ellice Islands comprises the world's fourth smallest country, now known as Tuvalu. The name means 'cluster of eight' in Tuvaluan though there are actually nine islands. Eight of these – Nanumaga, Niutao, Nanumea, Nukulaelae, Nui, Nukufetau, Vaitupu and Funafuti – have lagoons in the middle. The ninth and most southerly island – Niulakita – only has a swamp. Nobody lives there so it's not counted.* **4. ECUADOREAN VOLCANOES** Nine volcanoes surround Quito, the capital of Ecuador, which lies in the Avenue of Volcanoes, a 325 km valley between two massive ranges of the Andes. In Ecuador as a whole, there are 39 volcanoes, including Chimborazo (the world's highest inactive volcano) and Cotopaxi (the world's highest active one) but since records began with the Spanish invasion in 1534, only nine of them have erupted. The famous Galapagos Islands, an offshore province of Ecuador, are themselves the tops of huge underwater volcanoes. **5. EVILS** *In Bhutan, The Meeting of Nine Evils, or Ngenpa Guzom, is a public holiday. The Bhutanese believe nothing good can be achieved on this day. There is no merit in performing good deeds, and bad deeds produce really bad karma, so people minimise the risk by doing as little as they conceivably can. They stay indoors, if possible, eating and drinking. If they do go out, they never travel anywhere, but may indulge in a little light archery – Bhutan's national sport. In Dante's* The Divine Comedy *there were nine levels of Hell.* **6. EGYPTIAN AND ETRUSCAN GODS** The nine main gods of ancient Egypt were known as the Ennead, Greek for nine. Nun (water) had always existed. Then Atum (the sun) condensed out of the mist and sneezed, giving birth to Shu (air) and Tefnut (moisture). Tefnut and Shu gave birth to Geb (earth) and Nut (sky). The Etruscans (forerunners of the Romans) also had nine gods – Juno, Minerva, Tinia, Vulcan, Mars, Saturn, Hercules, Summanus and Vedius, immortalised in Macaulay's poem 'Horatius' (1842): 'Lars Porsena of Clusium, by the nine gods he swore...' **7. ENDINGS** *On the death of a pope, the cardinals celebrate a series of funeral masses for nine days. They are known as the 'Novemdiales.' The Aztecs believed that there were nine stages of the afterlife. Thomas Edison's favourite piece of poetry was the ninth verse of Thomas Gray's 'Elegy in a Country Churchyard'. He would recite it all the time: 'The boast of heraldry, the pomp of power, And all that beauty, all that wealth e'er gave, Awaits alike the inevitable hour: The paths of glory lead but to the grave.'* **8. ENIGMA VARIATIONS** Edward Elgar's *Enigma Variations* are said each to relate to how one of his friends would have played the music. The ninth, and perhaps most famous, variation, is called 'Nimrod', after the Old Testament patriarch described in the Bible as 'a mighty hunter'. It was named punningly for Elgar's best friend Augustus J. Jaeger, whose surname means 'hunter' in German. 'Nimrod' is always played at the Cenotaph in London on Remembrance Sunday. **9. EXTRAS** *The largest egg ever laid was by the extinct Great Elephant Bird (Aepyornis maximus). It had a volume of nine litres, equivalent to 15 dozen hen's eggs. Bodhidharma, the founder of Zen Buddhism, found enlightenment by sitting facing a wall on Mount Songshan in northern China for nine years. E999 is an extract from the bark of a South American tree. It is used as a foaming agent in ginger beer and cream soda, and by Andean Indians as cough mixture because it softens phlegm.*

# QI ANNUAL PUZZLE PAGE

1. Stare at the cross in the middle for about fifteen seconds, without looking away. Then, while continuing to stare at the cross, move your head towards and away from the page.

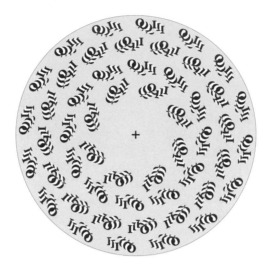

2. Stare at the three dots in the middle of this image for a full thirty seconds – don't let your eyes wander. Then look away at a bright surface, and keep watching for ten seconds. Don't worry – the ghostly image should go away sometime before you try to go to sleep...

3. Stare at the white dot in the middle of the first image for thirty seconds. No cheating or looking away. After the full thirty seconds, quickly move your focus to the same white dot in the middle of the second, black-and-white picture. It appears colourful until you move your focus even slightly.

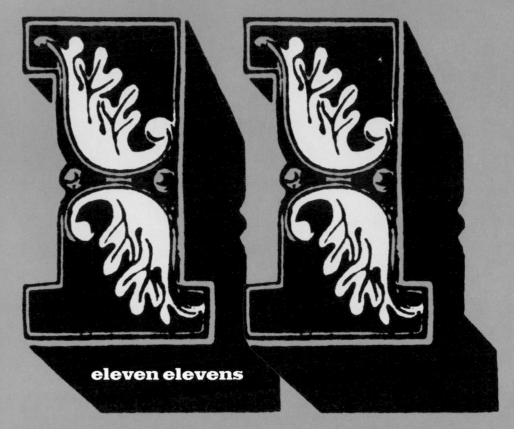

**eleven elevens**

*I've dealt with numbers all my life, of course, and after a while you begin to feel that each number has a personality of its own… Eleven is tough, an outdoorsman who likes tramping through woods and scaling mountains.*

PAUL AUSTER
*'The Music of Chance'*

**11** comes from the Old English word *endleofan*, which means 'one left'. When counting manually, it's what's left once you've used up all your fingers and thumbs. Twelve comes from *twelf*, meaning 'two left'. If the Inuit need to count to more than eleven, they have to do it in Danish.

**11** is the maximum number of times you can fold a piece of paper – not seven as popular wisdom has it. This was nailed early in 2007 by a team from the US TV show *Mythbusters*. They used a NASA hangar to make up a huge single sheet by sticking 17 rolls of paper together – the final dimensions were 170 x 220 feet. This was folded and folded, until it got stuck at 11 folds.

**11**+2 and 'eleven plus two' are both anagrams of 12 + 1 and 'twelve plus one'.

It's **11** million years since the relatives of the Laotian stone rat (*Laonastes aenigmamus* or 'enigmatic stone-dwelling mouse') wandered the earth. A specimen discovered hanging in a Laotian butchers in 1996 was subsequently confirmed, not only as a new species but the only living member of a rodent family that had been assumed extinct for aeons. The stone rat is easily mistaken for a grey squirrel, except for its limp tail and waddling, duck-like walk.

The German for **11** is *Elf*. So, in German-speaking Austria, ELF – the French brand of petrol – is called is ELAN. *Elan* is French for 'elk'.

Plovdiv, the second city of Bulgaria, has been renamed **11** times. The city has existed for 9,000 years, making it as old as Troy – and older than Athens or Rome. Its first name, whose origin is lost in the mists of history, was Kendros. The Thracians renamed it Eumolpias. It then became Philippopolis (Greek); Pulpudeva (Thracian again); Trimontium (Roman); Ulpia Thrimonzium

(Roman again); Pulden, Populdin, Ploudin (all Slavic); and Filibe (Turkish). It finally became Plovdiv after Bulgaria gained independence from Turkey in 1878. After which, the mainly Muslim population was subject to brutal ethnic cleansing. The remaining few, like the city itself, had to take Slavic names.

The deepest patch of sea is the Marianas Trench in the Pacific, off the coast of Guam. It is **11** kilometres (6.8 miles) deep. A coin dropped into it would take more than an hour to reach the bottom.

**11** days were lost when the Gregorian calendar was introduced into Britain in 1752. People went to bed on September 2nd and woke up on September 14th. This caused havoc. Contracts (and people's wages) were due to start on days that no longer existed.

General Antonio López de Santa Ana was President of Mexico **11** times between 1833 and 1855, during which he managed to lose more than half of the country's territory. Vain, corrupt and ruthless, he styled himself the 'Napoleon of the West', 'President for Life' and 'Serene Highness'. But he was a shrewd political operator and a great showman. In 1842, he had the leg he'd lost in a battle four years earlier dug up and paraded around Mexico City before mounting it in a shrine as testament to his heroism and courage.

Marilyn Monroe didn't have **11** toes. The rumour stems from a single photo taken on a beach in 1946 when she was still Norma Jean Dougherty. The 'extra toe' was just a lump of wet sand sticking to her foot. The photographer, Joseph Jasgur, invented the story as a publicity ruse for his 1991 book *The Birth of Marilyn: The Lost Photographs of Norma Jean.* He had noticed the 'extra toe' while preparing the original proofs over 40 years.

THE FIRST WORLD WAR ENDED AT THE *11TH* HOUR ON THE *11TH* DAY OF THE *11TH* MONTH OF 1918. NUMEROLOGISTS BELIEVE THAT EVENTS OCCUR AT *11:11* MORE REGULARLY THAN THEY SHOULD BY CHANCE ALONE. SINCE 9/11, THEY'VE BEEN WORKING OVERTIME. THE TWIN TOWERS FORMED AN *'11'* AND TOOK *11* YEARS TO BUILD; THE FIRST PLANE TO HIT WAS FLIGHT *11*; 9+1+1 = *11*; AND 'GEORGE W BUSH', 'MOHAMMED ATTA', 'NEW YORK CITY', 'THE PENTAGON' AND 'WAR DECLARED' ARE EACH FORMED FROM *11* LETTERS.

*Spooky eh? But then, the same goes for Jesus Christ, Harry Potter and Bart Simpson.*

# ENGLAND

*'There are many things in life more worthwhile than money. One is to be brought up in this our England, which is still the envy of less happy lands.'*

LORD DENNING Observer, 1968

England is about the same size as New York State – 74 times smaller than the USA, 59 times smaller than Australia and 3 times smaller than Japan. More than 83% of the people in the UK live in England, where the population density is 4 times that of France and more than 10 times that of the USA. More languages are spoken in England than in any other country in Europe. Over 300 different languages are spoken by London schoolchildren. From 1066 to 1362, the official language of England was French. England and Wales have the worst crime rate in the Western world. Every year, about 100 children in England and Wales are killed by their parents. The English consume a third of the world's tea exports. They drink more TEA than anyone else in the world: 2 ¹/₂ times as much as the Japanese and 22 times as much as the Americans or French. England is the world's oldest parliamentary democracy and the home of the world's oldest public zoo. 50% of English households have a pet and almost all of them have an MP.

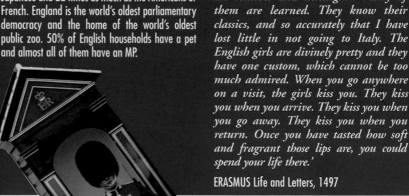

*'The air is soft and delicious. The men are sensible and intelligent. Many of them are learned. They know their classics, and so accurately that I have lost little in not going to Italy. The English girls are divinely pretty and they have one custom, which cannot be too much admired. When you go anywhere on a visit, the girls kiss you. They kiss you when you arrive. They kiss you when you go away. They kiss you when you return. Once you have tasted how soft and fragrant those lips are, you could spend your life there.'*

ERASMUS Life and Letters, 1497

# ECUADOR

Ecuador is the world's largest exporter of bananas, the world's largest exporter of the anti-malarial drug quinine and the world's largest source of balsa wood for model aircraft. Its next most important exports are oil, cut flowers and prawns. Panama hats all come from Ecuador. They were originally produced for export to workers on the Panama Canal. A good Panama hat can be rolled up, passed through a napkin ring and then reshaped perfectly, but locals turn their noses up at them, saying they are only for gringos: they prefer the classier Montecristo hat. Ecuador means 'equator' in Spanish. Ecuador's highest mountain, Chimborazo, was for a long time mistakenly believed to be the highest mountain in the Andes, which is strange, because at least 20 Andean peaks are taller.

On the other hand, because of the country's geographical position, even the beaches of Ecuador are further from the centre of the earth than the top of Mount Everest. Ecuador was originally called Quito, the name of its capital, the oldest in South America and the world's cheapest city to live in. It is said to have the best climate in the world. Quito is Spanish for 'I'm going' but it's actually named after the local Quitu indians.

Quito's proper name is San Francisco. Its full title is Villa de San Francisco de Quito ('the town of St Francis in Quito'). The state airline of Ecuador is called TAME. There are at least 1,500 different species of bird in Ecuador, including the oilbird, the world's only nocturnal fruit-eating bird, once melted down by the natives to make cooking oil. Over a million people in Ecuador speak Quechua, the language of the Incas, from which we get the words alpaca, coca, condor, guano, jerky, llama, pampas, puma and vicuna. George Lucas used it as the basis for Huttese, the language of Jabba the Hutt in *Return of the Jedi*.

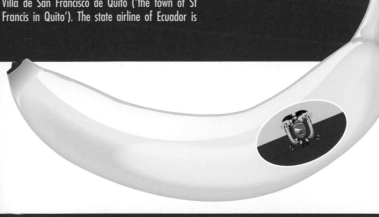

# EL SALVADOR

El Salvador is Spanish for 'The Saviour' and is named after Jesus Christ. It is the smallest country in Central America. It's also the most densely populated country on the mainland of either North or South America.

The most famous son of El Salvador was the Roman Catholic Archbishop Óscar Romero (1917–1980), revered locally as 'San Romero', the country's unofficial patron saint. In 1980, he spoke out in a sermon against the government, calling on soldiers to disobey orders that violated basic human rights.

Moments later, he was assassinated at the altar, his blood spilling into the communion wine. El Salvador's longest-serving president was General Maximiliano Hernández Martínez (1882–1966), the first of many such military men. He clung to power for 13 years. A keen spiritualist, he liked to say, 'It is a greater crime to kill an ant than a man,' on the grounds that human beings are reincarnated but an ant dies forever. No doubt he felt this justified massacring 40,000 peasants in an anti-Communist purge in 1932. Although an admirer of Hitler, he joined the Allies in World War Two and saved 40,000 Hungarian Jews by issuing passports to make them Salvadorean citizens. This meant they were not legal enemies of the Third Reich, entitling them to protection by the International Red Cross. El Salvador was the only country in the world to do this and never received (nor asked for) anything in return. Martínez was ousted from power in 1994, by which time Hungary had more Salvadorean citizens than all their other foreign nationals combined, though hardly any of them spoke Spanish or could point out El Salvador on a map. It is also the only Latin American nation to have sent troops into Iraq since the US-led invasion of 2003. At home, though, politics are more complicated. In the 1984 elections, a US $10 million computerised register was used – the old one had to be scrapped after it was found to contain 92,000 errors.

## The US Food and Drug Administration's permitted filth levels in food

**Broccoli (frozen)**
60 aphids and/or thrips and/or mites per 100 grams

**Curry Powder**
100 insect fragments per 25 grams
(+ 4 rodent hairs)

**Dates (chopped)**
5 whole insects (or the equivalent in dismembered ones) per 100 grams

**Hops**
2,500 aphids per 100 grams

**Mushrooms (dried)**
20 maggots and 75 mites per 15 grams

**Peanut Butter**
30 insect fragments per 100 grams (+ 1 rodent hair)

**Pepper (ground)**
475 insect fragments per 50 grams (+ 1 rodent hair)

**Pepper (whole)**
1 mg of mammal droppings per pound

**Pizza Sauce/Tomato Paste**
30 fruit fly eggs per 100 grams
OR 15 eggs and 1 maggot OR 2 maggots

**Raisins (golden)**
10 whole insects (or the equivalent in bits)
plus 35 fruit fly eggs per 8 oz

**Sauerkraut**
50 thrips per 100 grams

**Sesame Seeds**
5 mg of mammal droppings per pound

**Spinach (canned or frozen)**
50 aphids and/or thrips and/or mites per 100 grams

**Tomatoes (canned)**
10 fruit fly eggs per 500 grams
OR 5 eggs + 1 maggot OR 2 maggots

**Thyme (ground)**
925 insect fragments per 10 grams
(+ 2 rodent hairs)

**Wheat Flour**
75 insect fragments per 50 grams (+ 1 rodent hair)

## EINSTEIN

Albert Einstein (1879–1955) was dyslexic. He took so long learning how to talk, his parents thought he was retarded. He couldn't speak properly until he was nine. He also had a terrible memory and spent most of his childhood building card houses and doing jigsaw puzzles. He found school both boring and frightening, and at the age of twelve decided to dedicate his life to solving the riddle of the "huge world". He left school at 15, without a diploma, and the following year failed the entrance exam to Zurich Polytechnic. This was partly because he was lousy at French. When he finally got in he hated it so much that it put him off science for a whole year. In 1900, he scraped through the exams, afterwards working as a maths tutor and then as a patent clerk (third class) in Bern. He hated wearing socks and got his PhD for writing about how a cup of tea works.

$E=mc^2$

# PIECES OF EIGHT
### — OR —
## A Pirate's Life For Me
### BY CAPT$^N$ VIC REEVES

1. When Julius Caesar was captured by pirates, he treated them with utter contempt, told them to double his ransom and swore he would crucify them when they let him go. They thought he was joking. A few days after his release, he returned and kept his promise.

2. The pirate William Dampier (1652–1715) was the first European to see a kangaroo. He introduced many new words into English, including avocado, breadfruit, caress, cashew, chopsticks, petrel, posse, snug and barbecue (from the Arawak Indian word, *barbacoa*).

3. The French version of *barbacoa* was *boucan*, from which we get the word 'buccaneer'. French settlers on Hispaniola were called *boucaniers* because they lived by hunting and smoking pigs – until the Spaniards drove them out and forced them to take up piracy.

4. The Jolly Roger is first mentioned in *A General History of the Robberies and Murders of the most notorious Pyrates* (1724). It didn't always carry a skull and crossbones – Blackbeard's had a skeleton and a bleeding heart. Even more feared than the Jolly Roger was the 'Bloody Red', which signified that no life would be spared.

5. Most supposed pirate terms are pure fiction. Robert Louis Stevenson's *Treasure Island* (1883) introduced the black spot, the pirate map (with X marks the spot) and buried treasure. Even walking the plank seems to have been a myth: the only recorded case happened in 1829, well after most piracy had ceased.

6. Pirates didn't go 'Arrr!' Robert Newton, who played Long John Silver in the 1950 film of *Treasure Island*, started it. It wasn't even in the script, although 'avast', 'shiver my timbers!', 'yo-ho-ho' and 'matey' were.

7. The unique rongorongo script of Easter Island was the only written language to have existed in the whole of the Pacific before the 20th century. Only the island's chiefs could read it. In 1862, they were all kidnapped by Peruvian pirates and perished in Chilean guano mines, along with a third of the island's population and, of course, the language.

8. Blackbeard (Bristol-born Edward Teach) 'liked to put cannon fuses in his hair and beard and light them so that he looked like the devil'. The Chinese female pirate Ching Shih commanded 70,000 buccaneers on over 400 ships. But the most ruthless pirate of all was the Frenchman François l'Ollonais (see over).

# Bill Bailey's Embarrassingly Named Composers

**THE BLESSED ST NOTKER BABULUS ('ST NOTKER THE IDIOT')** WAS A SWISS MONK WHO WAS ONE OF THE PIONEERS OF THE GREGORIAN CHANT AND A FRIEND OF THE HOLY ROMAN EMPEROR CHARLES THE FAT, KNOWN IN GERMAN BY THE EVEN MORE EMBARRASSING NAME OF KARL DER DICKE.

Notker was born in about AD 840 and died on April 6th 912. He stuttered so much that the other monks named him Babulus ('The Stammerer'). Rather embarrassingly, this also means 'fool' in Latin. By way of apology, Pope Julius made him a saint 900 years after his death.

**V. G. BACKFART** (1507–1576) was born in Transylvania. Mrs and Mrs Backfart doubtless toyed with naming their son 'Very Good', but settled on Valentinus Graevius for obvious reasons. Backfart was a Polish-Hungarian composer who tried to wriggle out of his name by variously spelling it Bakfart, Bakfark, Bakfare, Backfarckh and Bekwark. He died of the plague in Padua in 1576.

**PHILIP GREELEY CLAPP** (1888–1954). The American composer Clapp was strongly influenced by Muck. Dr Karl Muck was conductor of the Boston Symphony Orchestra. Probably too embarrassed to carry on, he allowed Clapp to have a go.

**ANDREAS CRAPPIUS** (1542–1623). The talented son of Johannes Krapp, he disguised his name by translating it into Latin. His uncle Philipp (1497–1560) also changed his name – from Schwarzerd (the faintly lavatorial 'Black-soil') to its Greek equivalent, Melanchthon.

**DR WILLIAM CROTCH** (1775–1847) started playing with his father's organ at the age of two. His painting *View From Hurley Bottom* (1806, on paper) is in the Tate Gallery. He penned 'Lo, star-led chiefs Assyrian odours bring'. Theorists pore over his 'Experiment in Motivic Saturation'. There is a picture of him wearing a dress in the National Portrait Gallery.* He was a musical genius who played before the King and Queen at Buckingham Palace at 4, was Organist of Christ Church at 15, Oxford Professor of Music at 22 and the first President of the Royal Academy of Music (1822–1832). He wrote the chimes of Big Ben. (The original 'hour bell' is named after Benjamin Caunt, a 17-stone boxer. It weighed nearly 17 tonnes. The present one weighs 13 tonnes and has an 11-inch crack.)

**FERENC FARKAS** (1905–2000) was a distinguished Hungarian composer whose works include 60 songs under the collective title 'Play Up, Gipsy!'

**J.J. FUX** (1160–1741). Born into an obscure peasant family, Johann Joseph Fux rose to become Music Director at the Imperial Court of Emperor Leopold I, the highest musical position in Europe.

This meant that absolutely everybody knew his name. To make matters worse, Austria issued a Fux postage stamp in 1985.

**An embarrassing composer**

*Aged 3.

STOTEN

**BRIAN HAVERGAL** (1876–1972) lived to be 96, and wrote 32 symphonies.

**THOMAS-ANTOINE KUNTZ** (1756–1830) invented the orchestrion, a forerunner of the harmonium, in 1791. He was born Thomas Anton Kunz, but cleverly altered his name slightly so that no one would find it childishly amusing.

**LUIGI NONO** (1924–1990). The Italian Marxist composer Luigi Nono struggled on with the name he was born with, despite the fact that it allowed music critics to review every example of his work as 'another Nono'. Not known for easy listening, he set *The Communist Manifesto* and Viet Cong press releases to music and married Schoenberg's daughter Nuria. It's a pity he never wrote a nonet (a piece for nine players). If he had, it would have been known as a Nono Nonet.

**HEINRICH POOS** (1928–) is a contemporary German composer of Dutch descent. The name Poos is not embarrassing. It's Dutch for 'interval'.

EDMUND RUBBRA (1901–1986) was a working-class Buddhist from Northampton who was taught music by Gustav Holst. During the Second World War he formed a piano trio with two other spelling mistakes, Norbert Brainin and William Pleeth. He wrote 162 works, including 11 symphonies.

PETER SCHAT (1935–2003) of Utrecht was subject to the unwelcome attentions of Professor Fokker. Schat was an avant-garde composer. Fokker had a low opinion of his work, or Schit, as he called it. Stop tittering at the back, there. Schat is Dutch for 'sweetie-pie'.

LUDVIG THEODORE SCHYTTE (1848–1909). The Danish composer Schytte was born in Aarhus. He wrote '24 Little Fantasies'.

VLADISLAV SHOOT (1941–) narrowly avoided having an embarrassing name by being born in Vosnesensk in the Ukraine. He studied composition at the Gnesin Institute in Moscow and was music editor of *Sovetsky Kompositor* (1967–82). He now lives in Devon.

The composer and violinist JOSEPH SUK (1874–1935) was both the pupil and the son-in-law of Dvořák.

ANTON TITZ (1742–1810) was a German violinist and composer resident in Russia.

The Austrian composer HERBERT WILLI (b.1946) plays the Fagott.**

*This is a faggott*

You may also be unfamiliar with the oeuvres of ELSE AAS, JIRI BENDA, ROBERTA BITGOOD, LEO BLECH, DICK BOLKS, BENEDICTUS BUNS (1642–1716), POMPEYO CAMPS, ELI COFF, JEAN CRASS, ERIC FUNK, JESTER HAIRSTON, OSWALD JOOS, CYRILLIUS KREEK, CONRAD MAXIMILIEN KUNZ, JOHANN LICKL, WOUTER PAAP, GIUSEPPE MARIA PO, NICOLAS PONCE, HERMAN PYS, SAMUEL SCHEIDT, CORNELIUS SCHUYT, TIBOR SERLY, FERNANDO SOR and JOHANNES WORP.

*Pronunciation guide: Fux is pronounced Fooks; Kuntz and Kunz as Koonts; Suk is Sook. Manuel and Juan Ponce, being Spanish, are both pronounced Ponthay; Jose Pons, a Spaniard in Italy, is Ponz; the Swiss-Dutch composer Luctor Ponse (b.1914) is (tee hee) Ponce.*

**It's not what you think. Fagott is German for bassoon.

**Two young composers with names so embarrassing they can't be mentioned**

# EUROPEAN LANGUAGES
## No. 1: Turkish

The Turkish language can be conveniently (if fruitlessly) laid out in the following manner:

### 1. Turkish words that look like English but mean something entirely different

| | |
|---|---|
| arse | violin bow |
| bap | chapter |
| basin | the press |
| batman | thrust (as in a jet engine) |
| bay | gentleman |
| ben | I, myself. Also, a mole or beauty spot |
| bender | commercial port |
| berk | hard, firm, solid, strong, rugged |
| bet | face. Also, bad, ugly |
| bilge | learned, wise |
| bin | thousand; son of |
| bint | daughter; girl |
| bit | louse |
| bite | bollard |
| biz | we |
| bot | dinghy |
| bum | bang |
| fart | talking nonsense |
| zip | suddenly |
| zip! | pop! |
| zit | the opposite |

### 2. Turkish words that look quite like English but mean something entirely different

| | |
|---|---|
| bastarda | flagship |
| bok | shit |
| cok | many |
| erk | power, energy |
| kunt | thick |
| zonk zonk zonk | throbbing |

### 3. Turkish words that look like Belgian but mean something entirely different

| | |
|---|---|
| belge | document |

### 4. Turkish words that look like a Belgian speaking English but aren't

| | |
|---|---|
| zat | person, essence, substance, individual |
| zem | blame |

### 5. Very Turkish-sounding Turkish words

| | |
|---|---|
| zamazingo | mistress |
| zamir | inner consciousness |
| zulmen | cruelty |

### 6. Concepts uniquely expressible in a single word in Turkish

| | |
|---|---|
| bender | a fortress controlling the sea |
| bibi | a paternal aunt |
| bidik | short and plump |
| bingil bingil | quivering like a jelly (i.e. enormously fat) |
| bizbiz | a left-hand drumstick |
| sule | the blue part of a candle flame |
| yakmoez | the effect of moonlight sparkling on water |
| zebella | a huge, thickset man |
| zibidi | weirdly dressed |
| zilli | with bells on |
| zula | a secret store for smugglers or thieves |

### 7. Colourful idiomatic Turkish phrases

**zemzem kuyusana isemek**
to do something revolting just to get famous. Literally, 'to seek glory by urinating in the sacred well of Mecca'

# EIGHTEENTH-CENTURY CRIMINALS

*THE CRIMINAL CLASSES IN 18TH-CENTURY ENGLAND PRODUCED A VAST ARRAY OF SPECIALIST ROGUES.*

## RUFFLERS
WERE ARMED ROBBERS DISGUISED AS OUT-OF-WORK SOLDIERS.

## PRIGGERS
WERE EITHER MEMBERS OF A THREE-MAN SHOPLIFTING TEAM OR HORSE-THIEVES.

## SWADDLERS
NOT ONLY STOLE FROM THEIR VICTIMS BUT BEAT THEM UP AS WELL,
SOMETIMES MURDERING THEM INTO THE BARGAIN.

## SWIG-MEN
COVERED THEIR ROGUERY BY PRETENDING TO BE ITINERANT HABERDASHERS.

## STROWLERS
WERE CON MEN WHO CONVINCED COUNTRY GENTLEMEN TO 'LEND' THEM MONEY
SO THEY COULD GO TO LONDON.

## DOMMERERS
WERE BEGGARS POSING AS ESCAPED SLAVES WHO HAD HAD THEIR TONGUES CUT OUT BY THE TURKS
FOR REFUSING TO ACCEPT ISLAM.

## GLIMMERERS
WERE WOMEN WHO WENT AROUND IN FLOODS OF TEARS CLAIMING THAT THEIR HOUSES HAD BEEN BURNED DOWN.
ALTERNATIVELY, THEY SET OTHER PEOPLE'S HOUSES ON FIRE, IN ORDER TO LOOT THEM IN THE CONFUSION.

## BAWDY-BASKETS
WERE WOMEN POSING AS SELLERS OF PINS AND NEEDLES OR PORNOGRAPHIC BOOKS TO DISGUISE THEIR REAL GAME,
WHICH WAS STEALING LINEN CLOTHES OFF HEDGES.

## BULLY-HUFFS
HUNG ROUND BROTHELS, SURPRISING AND THREATENING THE CUSTOMERS BY CLAIMING
THAT THE WOMAN THEY WERE IN BED WITH WAS THEIR WIFE. IN BETWEEN TIMES, THEY INTERCEPTED LUCKY GAMBLERS
AS THEY LEFT THE CASINO TO RELIEVE THEM OF THEIR WINNINGS.

## BUFFER-NABBERS
WERE PROFESSIONAL DOG-THIEVES WHO KILLED THE ANIMAL TO SELL ITS SKIN.

## RUM-BUBBERS
SPECIALISED IN STEALING SILVER TANKARDS FROM TAVERNS
(not to be confused with rum-dubbers, who were run-of-the-mill lock-pickers).

## BUNG-NIPPERS
STOLE THE GOLD BUTTONS FROM CLOAKS AND THE SILVER TASSELS FROM HATBANDS.

## MUMPERS
WERE GENTEEL BEGGARS.

## CLAPPERDOGEONS
WERE PROFESSIONAL VAGABONDS, VARLETS WHO WORE PATCHED CLOAKS AND THREE HATS, ONE ON TOP OF THE OTHER.

## TATMONGERS
WERE CARD-SHARPS.

# Exclusive Clubs of the Eighteenth Century

**1. Name:** The Farting Club, Cripplegate
*Members:* Flatulent
*Activities:* Meeting once a week 'to poison the neighbourhood, and with their noisy crepitations attempt to outfart one another'.

**2. Name:** The Everlasting Club
*Members:* Bores
*Activities:* Sitting in a drinking session for twenty-four hours a day, 'no person presuming to rise until he was relieved by his appointed successor'.

**3. Name:** The Humdrum Club
*Members:* 'Gentlemen of peaceable dispositions'
*Activities:* 'Meet at a tavern, smoke pipes and say nothing till midnight'.

**4. Name:** The Surly Club, Billingsgate
*Members:* Tradesmen
*Activities:* 'To sharpen the practice of contradiction and of foul language'.

**5. Name:** Beefsteak Club
*Members:* Politicians and wits
*Activities:* 'Devoted to drinking and wit interspersed with snatches of song and much personal abuse'.
(Rivals: The Sublime Society of Steaks)

**6. Name:** Kit-Kat Club, Shire Lane
*Members:* Leading Whigs
*Activities:* Toasting beautiful women and eating pies.

**7. Name:** Twopenny Club
*Members:* Poor men
*Activities:* 'If any neighbour swears or curses, his neighbour may give him a kick upon the shin'.

**8. Name:** The No-Nose Club
*Members:* Unknown
*Activities:* Unknown.

**9. Name:** The Club of Broken Shopkeepers, Southwark
*Members:* Bankrupts
*Activities:* Cheap drinking.

**10. Name:** The Man-Killing Club, St Clement Danes
*Members:* Anonymous
*Activities:* Membership barred to anyone 'who had not killed his man'.

**11. Name:** The Mock Heroes Club
*Members:* Fantasists
*Activities:* 'Each member would assume the name of a defunct hero'.

**12. Name:** The Lying Club, Westminster
*Members:* Wags
*Activities:* 'Members were banned from uttering any true word'.

**13. Name:** The Golden Fleece
*Members:* Amusing drunks
*Activities:* Inventing names such as Sir Boozy Prate-All, Sir Whore-Hunter and Sir Ollie-Mollie.

# DARA O'BRIAIN'S
# IRE

Mary had not suffered herself as she was an 'asymptomatic' carrier of the disease, possibly from before birth, and this all occurred during that awkward time in history, before we knew what an asymptomatic carrier of a disease is, and how they should be quarantined, but after the time where we happily burned people for being witches just because their last five jobs ended in houses filled with wheezing, dying people. And either of those solutions would have been better from a public health viewpoint than just sending Madge back to the temping agency for another go.

She was sent into compulsory quarantine twice; the second time for life. Which seems harsh, but she was only released from the first quarantine under strict instructions that she never work with food again. Our heroine then changed her name to Mary Brown and got a job in New York's Sloan Hospital, working in (surprise, surprise) the kitchens. Man, that Mary just loves to cook. 25 more people were infected.

She lived out the rest of her days on North Brother Island on the East River and became something of a celebrity at the time, regularly interviewed by journalists. These days she'd probably bring out a celebrity diet cookbook and get sworn at by Gordon Ramsay.

She died of pneumonia in 1938, and an autopsy found typhoid bacteria in her gallbladder. They cremated her. Twice, probably.

**Burke and Hare** – *If I said you had a beautiful body, would you sell it to me for £15?*

The history of effective medicine is surprisingly short. Only 300 years ago it was still blood-letting, leeches and homeopathy. Luckily, none of that nonsense remains today.

Surgeons began as barbers (this is the reason qualified surgeons are still called Mr rather than Dr in deference to their lowly beginnings) and medicine only started coming on in leaps and bounds when they stopped thinking it was all about imbalances in your bile and phlegm and started cutting people up and having a look. But where to get the bodies? Well, if it's 1827 and you're Edinburgh anatomist Prof. Robert Knox you naturally pay two Irish lads when they turn up at your doorstep with the corpse of a man who owed one of them £4 rent. And you don't ask questions, neither. You just hand over £7 and start slicing. For Burke and Hare this was a clear £3 profit. And in such moments are great entrepreneurs born.

The following 11 months led to 16 further instances of supply and demand, where the two lads delivered to Knox sickly tenants, prostitutes, beggars, acquaintances and a mother and daughter two-for-one.

**AS IRISH AMBASSADOR TO QI, here's a golden opportunity to bore you senseless with some stuff about our Nobel Laureates. We get them so often I'm tempted to bang this piece through the spell-checker and send it to Stockholm just in case it's my turn. Four for Literature alone: Britain, with 15 times the population, only has six. We've even won a couple of Peace Prizes, which is quality since it was our war in the first place.**

**We've not won for Medicine, mind you – the forgotten Nobel, I always feel, especially in pub quizzes, much like Aston Villa winning the European Cup – despite some quite astonishing contributions to the world of health.**

## Irish Pioneers of Medicine, I salute you!

**Typhoid Mary** – *Now wash your hands*

Born Mary Mallon in Ireland in September 1869, and moving to New York at 15, The Typher was a domestic cook with a poor head for spotting co-incidences. 'Wow,' she would never say, **'All these people have caught typhoid! That's just what happened in my last five jobs! I really am unlucky in my choice of employers. Better get that CV out again.'** Over the course of her career she managed to infect 53 people with typhoid, all but the first batch of whom should probably have been a bit more thorough on the old **'And why did you leave your last job?'** question.

Her first job lasted only two weeks before typhoid struck. Her next gig led to fevers, diarrhoea and the laundress dying. She then went to work for a lawyer and gave seven of the eight members of the household the disease. Moving to a job in Long Island, within the fortnight, six more were laid up. Three more households were to become infected before fingers finally began to point.

And did she not like being accused of spreading disease! Jesus, she did not. She got quite tetchy about it. Even when she had been written up in the *Journal of the American Medical Association* she still wouldn't play ball. After all, she hadn't ever even had typhoid!

"TYPHOID MARY"

HARE

BURKE

In at least two of these instances, the medical students recognised the bodies placed before them for dissection but clearly Knox was quite the talker. Plus, it's said that he took the precaution of dissecting the face first. There's a good reason CSI isn't set in Edinburgh in 1827: 'We can't recognise the face.' 'Well, then you're free to go sir. Sorry for wasting your time. Oh and don't forget to take the rest of your cadaver with you on the way out. After all, it's probably worth a few quid.'

The business language I'm using here is not inappropriate: Knox paid more for fresher corpses. And the boys further boosted their profits by killing most of their victims by strangulation, in an effort to present the most usable body.

Burke and Hare were finally caught out when two other tenants in Hare's boarding house found a tiny fragment of incriminating evidence: a freshly killed body hidden under one of the beds. Even so, between alerting the police and the fuzz arriving to search the house, B&H still managed to sell the body to Knox yet again.

They later broke under questioning though, the body was identified and they were brought to trial. There was a final twist however. Without sufficient evidence to prosecute them, Hare was offered immunity to testify against Burke. His testimony led to Burke's hanging in 1829.

*That's not the twist though, this is the twist…*

Burke's body was then used by Edinburgh medical students for anatomy lessons. What a quality twist! What a dazzling irony! What a brilliant final shot!

We start on the dead face of Burke, the hangman's rope barely eased… and the camera pulls out. We see the scalpel lowered to his chest as a voice calmly says, 'If we make our initial incision here…' and as the camera continues to pull out we see a professor surrounded by white coated students… as the blade makes contact and the skin is opened, the students lean in, obscuring the view of the body. The camera continues to pull out over the class room, up and out through the bright windows, into the bright Edinburgh streets and out across the city. The End. Roll credits. The audience stumble out into the streets, frightened certainly, but still, reassured by such top-quality screenwriting.

Hare doesn't feature in the ending, by the way, because after he was released, he disappeared, his last known sighting being in Carlisle.

Prof. Knox was never found guilty of any crime, but his career understandably stalled in Edinburgh and he later moved to the London Cancer Hospital.

In 1832, the Anatomy Act was passed to supply cadavers legally for medical education about which *The Lancet* wrote, 'Burke and Hare… are the real authors of the measure.'

And Burke can still be seen, partly. After the dissection of his body, his skin was used to create the binding of a book, still on view in the excellent, and intermittently gruesome, museum at the Royal College of Surgeons of Edinburgh.

I've seen it. Disappointingly, it just looks like a book. It hasn't got an ear on the cover or anything.

## EUROPEAN LANGUAGES

### No. 2: Irish

My one claim to originality amongst Irishmen is that I have never made a speech.
GEORGE MOORE (1852–1933)

**Dublin is Irish for Blackpool.**

In Irish, fear means man and bean means woman. Fear used as a noun means 'man'; used as a verb it means to 'wage' (as in war). From bean we get the word banshee (bean sí : 'woman of the fairies'). The literal translation of the Irish word for jellyfish is 'seal-snot'.

Irish, also known as Gaelic, has the oldest literature in Europe apart from Latin or Greek.

Irish has been compulsory in schools in the Republic since independence in 1922. In surveys, between 1,000,000 and 500,000 people claim to speak it. They're lying. Out of a total population of 3.5 million, only about 50,000 people speak Irish with any degree of fluency, and less than 20,000 speak it like a native. There is only one weekly newspaper in Irish. It's called *Anois* and has a circulation of 5,000. Compare this to Wales where 10 times as many people speak Welsh. There are 500,000 fluent Welsh speakers out of a population of 2.9 million.

In Ireland, it is your legal right to have a speeding ticket served on you in Irish. To avoid being fined, speak nothing but Irish to the policeman. The chances are he won't be able to remember enough schoolboy Irish to complete the procedure.

It's often said that if the Irish government really wanted to have Irish widely spoken in Ireland, they should have forbidden it.

*IRISH DICTIONARY:* SOME INTERESTING SUB-DIVISIONS OF THE IRISH LANGUAGE ARE:

**1. Irish words that look exactly like English words but aren't**

| | |
|---|---|
| ball | member |
| bang | swimming stroke |
| beach | bee |
| bean | woman |
| biog | chirp |
| bob | trick |
| bod | penis |
| bog | to move |
| both | hut |
| brá | hostage |
| bran | raven, bream, bran |
| brat | cloak |
| bun | bottom |
| cab | gob |
| cabhailt | torso |
| cad? | what? |
| can | to sing or speak |
| cart | to scrape clean |
| clip | tease, torment |
| clog | clock, blister |
| corn | cup |
| corn | to coil |
| cos | foot, leg |
| crap | to shrink |
| go | to, that, until, well, and |
| gó | undoubtedly |
| gob | a bird's beak |
| mac | son |
| sin | that |

**2. Irish words that look like English names but aren't**

| | |
|---|---|
| beith | being, entity, birch |
| bri | meaning, significance |
| cath | battle |
| gus | courage |

**3. Irish words that look like French but aren't**

| | |
|---|---|
| bac | hindrance |
| bain | remove |
| bås | death |
| bis | vice |
| bord | table |
| cas | twist |
| col | aversion |

**4. Irish words that look like French and are**

| | |
|---|---|
| banc | bank |

**5. Irish words that look like Italian but aren't**

| | |
|---|---|
| båsta | waist |

**6. Irish words that look like German but aren't**

| | |
|---|---|
| bonn | sole of shoe, coin |

**7. Irish words that look like Spanish but aren't**

| | |
|---|---|
| cáca | cake |

**8. Irish words that look like Icelandic but aren't**

| | |
|---|---|
| brillin | clitoris |

**9. Irish words that look like Finnish but aren't**

| | |
|---|---|
| clapsholas | twilight |

**10. Ludicrously long Irish words with impossibly complicated spelling**

| | |
|---|---|
| caoinfhulangach | tolerant |
| cnuasainmneacha | collective nouns |
| comhaimsearthacht | contemporaneity |
| comhbhraíthreachas | confraternity |
| comhchoibhneasach | correlative |
| réamhchoinníôllacha | precondition |

**11. Irish words that look disgusting or sinister but turn out not to be**

| | |
|---|---|
| bangharda | policewoman |
| bothóg | shanty, cabin |
| bumbóg | bumblebee |
| cathair | city |
| deathoil | goodwill |
| fear gorm | black man |
| gorm | blue (or black when referring to skin) |

# CLARKSON'S edible environment

*SOMETIMES, AS I TRAVEL THE WORLD IN MY ENORMOUS CAR, I GLIMPSE NATURE THROUGH THE WINDSCREEN. THIS MAKES ME FEEL PECKISH. IF NO DECENT RESTAURANT IS AVAILABLE, I TEND TO LUNCH OFF THE LAND. HERE ARE SOME FAVOURITES.*

**Alligators** The edible bit is the tail, roasted or fried. The meat is flaky and tastes like chicken. Or veal. Or crocodile.

**Ants** Bit fiddly if you're in a hurry. Can be mashed to a pulp then dried and used to thicken soup. Dried, powdered ant keeps for ages. Roasted leafcutter ant abdomens are sold in cinemas in South America instead of popcorn. In Mexico, *escamoles* (ant pupae) are on the menu in the finest restaurants, fried in butter, or with onions and garlic. Ants should be cooked for at least 6 minutes to remove formic acid.

*Something from my glove compartment*

**Badgers** are related to skunks and polecats, but young badger tastes like pork. In the 18th century, salted spit-roasted badger was a treat for peasants.

**Barnacles** are chewed with pleasure in Portugal, Spain and Chile and by American Indians of the Pacific Northwest.

**Bats** should be disembowelled, then skinned like a rabbit after removing their wings and legs. Catch them by knocking them off their roosts with a stick while asleep during the day. The tastiest are plump fruit bats.

**Beavers** secrete aspirin through their skin, so may be good for headaches or stomach pains: especially those caused by eating bats. The best part of a beaver to eat is its scaly, paddle-like tail.

**Bees** are edible at all stages in their life cycle – pupa, larva and adult. Remove legs, wings and stings before roasting or boiling.

**Bird's dribble** is the sole ingredient of Chinese bird's nest soup, which is made entirely from the spittle of the Asian cave swift.

**Caterpillars** Over 30 species are eaten in the Democratic Republic of the Congo. You can get tinned caterpillars in Botswana and South Africa.

**Cats** Domestic cats are perfectly edible. Lions and tigers too, provided they don't eat you first. A bit on the stringy side, though. Stew thoroughly.

**Cicadas** were a favourite of the ancient Greeks. Aristotle recommended fried pregnant cicadas as a particular titbit.

*On the stringy side*

**Cockroaches** are a perennial treat in Belize, where roasted mashed roaches make up *cena molida* ('crushed supper' in Spanish).

**Dogs** are a delicacy in Korea, but also, as is less well known, in Switzerland. Wild dogs, foxes and wolves are impossible to stalk, but you may be able to lure them towards you by going about on all fours so that they think they're stalking you. Meat can be gristly. Remove anal glands.

**Dormice** fattened up by feeding them nuts and cooked in honey were a favourite of the ancient Romans.

**Dragonflies** are a popular dainty in Laos, Japan, Korea and Bali with coconut milk, ginger, garlic or shallots. Or try them plain-grilled and crispy.

**Grasshoppers** may be roasted or sautéed. Remove the wings and legs and season with onion, garlic, cayenne, chilli peppers or soy sauce. Candied grasshoppers, or *inago*, are a favourite cocktail appetiser in Japan.

**Guinea pigs** are enjoyed all over Peru and make good eating. In the cathedral at Cuzco, there is a painting of the Last Supper where Christ and his disciples are shown tucking into roast guinea pig.

**Hornets** are absolutely wolfed down in the remote mountain villages of Japan, where the giant variety are part of the staple diet. They are eaten deep-fried, or raw, as hornet sashimi. There are two main types: nocturnal and diurnal. Day hornets should be collected at night. Night hornets (which are collected by day) have a sting that has been likened to a white-hot rivet being driven into the body. They usually attack the face. *Bon appétit!*

**Hyenas** in ancient Egypt were fattened for the dinner table, but nobody enjoyed them much. Boil thoroughly to remove parasites.

**Insects** are more nutritious than vegetables – rich in fat, carbohydrates and protein – especially their succulent grubs. Beetle grubs can be larger than sausages, up to 7 inches long. Most insects are better for you if eaten raw, but taste better if cooked. Boiling is best, but roasting is easier. If you haven't got a saucepan, place them on hot stones or the embers of a fire. To eat a hairy caterpillar, squeeze it to remove its innards. Don't eat the skin. Nasty.

*Congolese rat recipe. Soak 12 small smoked field-rats in water for 30 minutes. Cook tomato, onion, pimento and palm oil in a large pan. Drain rats and skin. Remove any other inedible parts (your choice). Fry for 20 minutes, turning occasionally. Eat piping hot, bones and all. Serve as hors d'oeuvres.*

**Owls** are a protected species, and both the Bible and the Koran forbid eating them. But folk wisdom says that if a woman feeds her husband roast owl, he will become subservient to her every wish. No doubt this is why owl is all the rage in China. Chan Chen Hei, 52, a top Cantonese chef in Singapore, says owl is the best meat in the world to make soup with – better than chicken, pork, snake or turtle – but the smell can permeate the entire restaurant. He advises sealing the gap under the kitchen door with wet towels to prevent the stench escaping. Few people other than the Chinese, the Eskimos and the good folk of Louisiana eat owls for pleasure, but they've often been used for medicinal reasons. In medieval England, owl broth was given for whooping cough. The Romans thought it cured epilepsy whereas in India it was only good for rheumatism. For epilepsy, stewed owls' eyeballs were the thing. Mixed with owls' brains, they were also said to reduce labour pains. In 16th-century Switzerland, jellied owl brains in seawater were recommended for constipation. They weren't eaten, though, because that would have been silly. They were popped up the bottom.

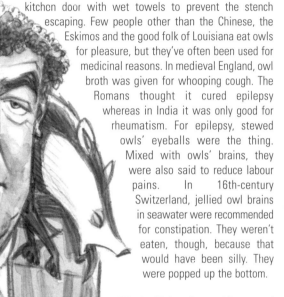

**Pigs' milk** is twice as rich as cows' milk, but difficult to get hold of. Cows produce milk for ten minutes at a time but pigs can only manage it for 15 seconds. Pigs have 14 small nipples all down their belly, whereas cows have four huge nipples conveniently clumped together. No one has so far devised a successful pig-milking machine. But perhaps their heart wasn't in it.

**Porcupines** are a delicacy in Gabon, Sudan, Nigeria, Ghana, Cameroon and in India, where they are compared to (and preferred to) pork. Malaysian porcupine curry is rather good. In Thailand, porcupine is barbecued with garlic, pepper and salt. It tastes like duck, only crunchier.

**Rabbits** Young rabbits often lie quite still and can be harvested simply by picking them up. Watch it, though: their flesh lacks fat and vitamins. Trappers in Canada literally ate themselves to death this way. The body uses its own

# CLARKSON'S CHOICE!

*Earthworms are extremely nutritious, very low in fat and 60 – 70% top-quality protein. Eating worms is a key survival skill for soldiers trapped in enemy territory. If forced to eat them raw, they should be starved for a day and then squeezed to remove any grit or poo. Raw, untreated worms taste like dirt. After starving and squeezing they taste like worm. This is barely an improvement.*

*If not a soldier in enemy territory but an ordinary, worm-eating civilian, purge your earthworms by soaking them in water overnight. This causes them to defecate. You may need to squeeze them to help the process along. Next wipe their bottoms and wash them in cold water. Plunge the live worms into boiling water and cook for 15 minutes. Drain. Boil again in fresh water at least once more, to remove all the mucus from their bodies.*

*After boiling they can be chopped and used in casseroles instead of chicken or beef. For oven-baked worms, freeze them to death. This stops them from wriggling off the baking tray. Defrost thoroughly, and bake in the oven at 200 degrees F for 30 minutes. The dried worms can be ground into a protein-rich meal and used instead of flour to make bread or cakes. Dried chopped worms can also be used instead of raisins or nuts. Mmmm.*

*The gourmet worm-fan will want The Worm Book by Loren Nancarrow and Janet Taylor. Try Worm 'N' Apple Cake, Apricot-Earthworm Balls and Oatmeal Earthworm-Raisin Muffins. NB Many of these contain eggs and cheese (as well as earthworms), so are not suitable for vegans.*

vitamins and minerals digesting rabbit, which are then excreted in the faeces. The more rabbit is eaten, the worse the deficiency becomes. People who eat nothing but rabbit will starve to death. Eating vegetation of any kind would have allowed the trappers to survive, but it was all buried under the snow.

*Don't eat insects that are sick or dead; that smell bad; that feed on carrion or dung; that produce a skin rash when handled; or that are brightly coloured. Everything else is yummy.*

**Rats** Live rats in the Guangxi Zhuang region of China cost 50 cents a pound, almost as much as chicken. Marinated rat steak from Fujian is said to be the best in the world. When gutting a rat be careful not to split its innards.

**Scorpions** In southern China, scorpions are reared in 'ranches' in people's homes, then sold in the markets. They have a woody taste and are eaten whole, except for the tail. Obviously. Scorpion soup, with pork, dates and berries, is nicer than toilet water from a motorway service station. In my view.

**Seagulls** Well, why not? First trap your seagull by wrapping food round a stone and throwing it in the air. The gull swallows the bait while still in flight, but the weight of the stone causes it to crash-land. It should be despatched as soon as you catch it in case it learns to take off with the new payload aboard. This method is best used over land. At sea, if you have a fishing rod handy, the ability of gulls to catch food in mid-air can be even more easily exploited by baiting a hook and casting it into the sky. Reel in and despatch by hand.

*Puddings are for girls*

**Slugs** are just snails covered with mucus instead of a shell. What's not to like? Try them seethed in milk, Italian-style. *The Best Washington State Slug Recipes* by Frank Howard is the 3,156,355th best-selling book on Amazon.

> *Porcupines are the most delicious and tender of all game animals. Do not skin them: the skin is the best part (rather like crackling). Pluck out the large quills then drop the animal into boiling water. Scrape the remaining feathery quills off. It will now look like a suckling pig with feet closely resembling a human hand. Set the feet aside. Remove entrails, head and anal scent glands, stuff with rice and dried fruit and leave in fridge overnight. Grease skin. Bake in oven until golden brown. When your guests ask what they're eating, produce one of the 'hands' and watch the reaction!*

**Snakes** Human beings all over the world eat snakes wherever they are found. I know I do. They are quite safe as long as you don't eat the head. Grass snakes in France are known as *anguilles de haie* ('hedge-eels'); the Japanese prefer sea snakes. In Oxfordshire, we make vipers into soup.

**Spiders** Large, tarantula-like varieties are particularly sought after in northern Cambodia and New Guinea. They taste like peanut butter. The Indians of French Guiana grill giant bird-eating spiders after plunging them in boiling water to remove the hairs. To make spider egg omelette, squeeze eggs out of spider onto a leaf and then smoke. Eat with tiny, tiny chips.

**Termites** can be boiled, fried or roasted, but are better for you if eaten raw. Termite meat has twice the protein of sirloin steak. They are widely eaten in Africa where they are lured by candlelight. Break the wings off before frying – delicious! The enormous termite queens are a special treat and are often reserved for children or grandparents, unless I can get there first.

**Warthogs** have been described as 'hideously grotesque long-legged pigs'. Their heads are covered with long blunt warts strengthened by gristle and they can be cooked in any of the ways suitable for cooking pork. But they don't taste like pork. Oh no. The chefs on South African Airlines recommend warthog terrine. Very smooth yet delightfully warty.

**Wasps** Most normal people (like me) remove legs, wings and sting before roasting or boiling, but canned whole wasps, wings and all, are sold in Japan. Wasp pupae are enjoyed in the inland region of Nagano as a substitute for fish. Rice cooked with wasps was a favourite dish of the Emperor Hirohito.

**Whale** was served for school lunches in Japan between 1945 and 1962, but most young people there have never tasted it. Traditionally eaten only in coastal whaling towns (and by gourmets in cities), after WWII food shortages led to the occupying US forces allowing the Japanese to hunt whales. By the early sixties, they had done this so effectively that there were very few whales left in the seas around Japan and consumption declined. Whale milk is as thick as cottage cheese, so it doesn't dissolve in water if it gets spilt. In the 19th century, the Tillamook Indians of Oregon ate blubber from whales washed ashore in Tillamook Bay. Their legends say that, in olden times, the whales cruised into the bay to be milked. It's thought that waxy lumps found along the shore may be petrified whale-milk cheese.

**Witchetty grubs** Large, white, wood-boring larvae of various moths are a popular snack in Australia. Skilled hunters can pluck the grub from its hole without 'spilling the gravy'. Eaten raw or roasted, they have a rich, nutty flavour, mainly because they are full of half-digested sawdust.

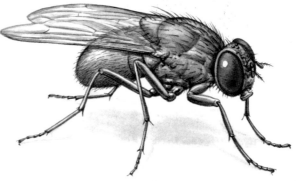

*I've seen more meat on a butcher's biro.*

*Selecting a ripe frog*

ENGLISH VILLAGES

BUCKY WATERS?

# Big Phill's ENGLISH VILLAGE Game

**It's often struck me that the average English village sounds more like an American sports commentator or news anchor than a place.**

Driving through this green and pleasant land, I find myself barking out lines like 'This is Fenny Bentley and Brant Broughton with *The News at Nine*' or 'This has been *Volleyball Tonight* – I'm Betton Strange' or '*Good Morning Albuquerque*, with Mansell Grange, Hoo Meavy, Nelson Rotman, Roseberry Topping, Toller Whelme, Rumbles Moor, Stanley Pontlarge and Scott Willoughby'.

See if you can tell which of these villages is actually a famous US TV personality, and which gritty-sounding bloke is really a sweet little English village.

| Danby Wiske | Verne Langdon | Marston Thrussell | Tedstone Delamere | Yardley Hastings | Gideon Yago | Harley Brinsfield | Nelson Burton |

## Which of these is a famous American TV personality?

(a) Devin Scillian
(b) Regis Cordic
(c) Cawood Ledford
(d) George Nympton
(e) Sway Calloway
(f) Mort Crim
(g) Brant Hansen
(h) Spero Dedes
(i) Bucky Waters
(j) Neda Ulaby
(k) Hilliard Gates
(l) Nachum Segal

## And can you spot the English Village?

(a) Patrick Brompton
(b) Shudy Camps
(c) Chaldon Herring
(d) Cary Lytes
(e) Charley Knoll
(f) Bentley Pauncefoot
(g) Bradford Bryan
(h) Clifford Chambers
(i) Newbold Saucy
(j) Curry Load
(k) Kex Beck
(l) Kirk Hallam

(Answers opposite)

AMERICAN TV PERSONALITIES

BENTLEY PAUNCEFOOT?

ANGER

FEAR

GRIEF

LOVE

JEALOUSY

# Emotions

Given the daily range, variety and power of human emotional experience, there has been surprisingly little research into the subject.

According to ancient Chinese philosophy there are only five basic emotions: ANGER, FEAR, GRIEF, LOVE AND JEALOUSY. These are subtly demonstrated on the left.

Paul Ekman, who studied the remote, Stone-Age Fore tribe of Papua New Guinea, also concluded that there are only five, but came up with a different list: ANGER, FEAR, SADNESS, HAPPINESS AND DISGUST.

One of the most influential people in the field is Robert Plutchnik, who identifies eight primary human emotions: ANGER, FEAR, SADNESS, DISGUST, SURPRISE, CURIOSITY, ACCEPTANCE AND JOY.

At QI, however, we think there are a lot more emotions than eight, including:

| | |
|---|---|
| ANGUISH | LAZINESS |
| ANXIETY | LONELINESS |
| BAFFLEMENT | LUST |
| BITTERNESS | MISCHIEVOUSNESS |
| CERTAINTY | MISERY |
| CHAGRIN | NARCISSISM |
| CHEERFULNESS | NONCHALANCE |
| COMPASSION | OBSEQUIOUSNESS |
| CONTEMPT | PANIC |
| CONTENTMENT | PETULANCE |
| CRUELTY | PLAYFULNESS |
| CURMUDGEONLINESS | POIGNANCY |
| CYNICISM | RELIEF |
| DELIGHT | REMORSE |
| DETERMINATION | SCHADENFREUDE |
| DISCOMFITURE | SELF-CONFIDENCE |
| DISTRUST | SELF-SATISFACTION |
| DOUBT | SHAME |
| EMPATHY | SHOCK |
| EXCITEMENT | STINGINESS |
| FOREBODING | STUBBORNNESS |
| FORGIVENESS | SUSPICION |
| FRUSTRATION | SYMPATHY |
| GLOOM | TENDERNESS |
| HARD-HEARTEDNESS | TORPOR |
| HATRED | VANITY |
| HOMESICKNESS | VEHEMENCE |
| HORROR | VENERATION |
| HUBRIS | VENGEFULNESS |
| INDECISION | WARINESS |
| INDIFFERENCE | WARMTH |
| INDIGNATION | WISTFULNESS |
| IRRITABILITY | WORLD-WEARINESS |
| JOLLITY | and WORRY |

PLUS twenty more lavishly exemplified on the right.

# Words With No
# English Equivalents

Would you care for jam Sir?

**Kouloúra**
(Greek: a ring shaped loaf of bread or a lavatory seat)

**Manjan**
(Malay: to rove in quest of girls)

Sorry, you can't come in here, you're not wearing a dog

**Ikkuserpok**
(Inuit: to tie one leg of a dog to one's neck)

Song! Song!

**Song**
(Malay: call to an elephant to lift one leg)

An amusingly horrid little wine don't you think?

**Dreimannerwein**
(German: a wine so disgusting it takes three men to make you drink it)

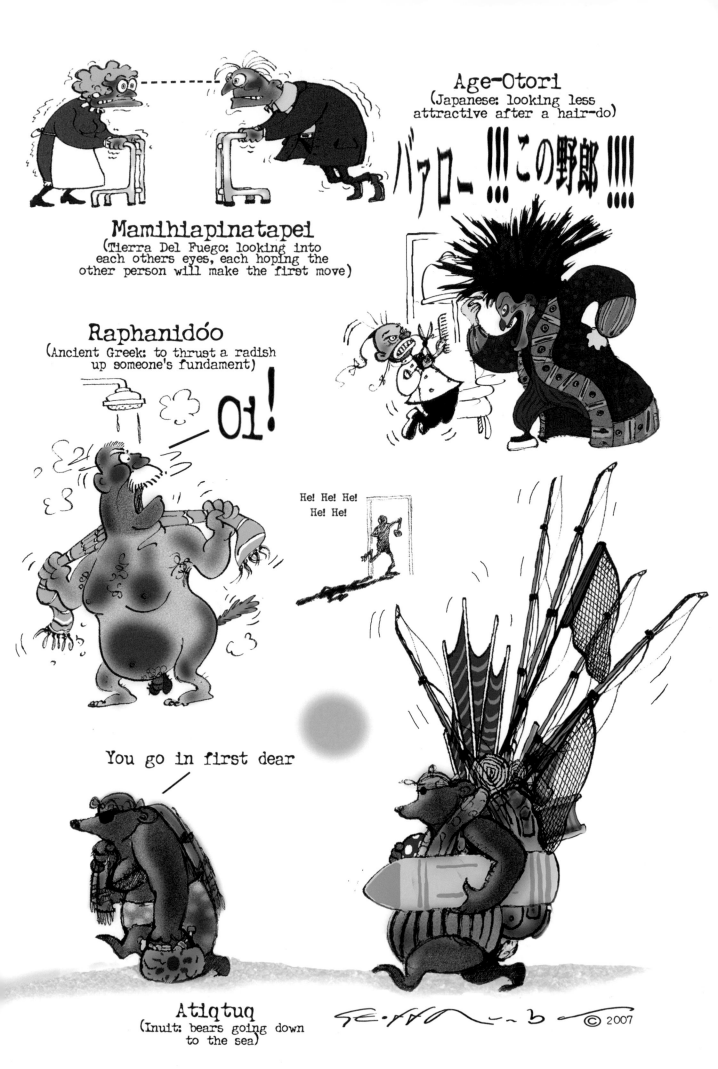

# THE ENGLISH ELM by CLIVE ANDERSON

SINCE BOTH WORDS BEGIN WITH E, ENGLISH ELMS ARE A PERFECT SUBJECT FOR THIS BOOK. PERFECT FOR ME, CERTAINLY, AS I'M PRESIDENT OF THE WOODLAND TRUST, A CHARITY WHOSE AIM IS TO PRESERVE ANCIENT WOODLAND AND PLANT MORE NATIVE BRITISH TREES *(POSSIBLE MOTTO: 'BRING BACK THE BIRCH').*

## TREES ARE US

Europe as a whole has about 250 native tree species, which makes Britain's 30-something look very puny. Even 250 is nothing when compared to the tree-rich rain forests of the tropics where hundreds of species grow in a single acre – assuming, that is, they haven't all been chopped down by the time you read this.

## THE 'ENGLISH' ELM

*Ulmus procera* (Latin for 'foremost elm') has been known as the 'English Elm' for centuries. This doesn't necessarily mean anything. There are no lions running around Britain, but that hasn't stopped them being adopted as our national symbol – the result, perhaps, of Scottish lions rampant getting into bed with English lions couchant. And, in fact, it seems that, though English Elms have been living – and dying – in our woods and hedgerows for centuries, most experts agree they did not grow in this country until they were brought here from continental Europe. Just when that happened is not clear, but it seems certain that the English Elm is not, in fact, English.

## THERE'LL ALWAYS BE AN ENGLAND

Several tree species are called 'English', notably the English Oak *(Quercus robur)*. It's one of only two species of oak (of which there are hundreds worldwide) native to Britain. Also snappily known as the pedunculate oak, it's common to many parts of Europe. But, in some corner of a foreign field, it is forever English to us. Much the same is true of the English Yew. The Scots Pine *(Pinus sylvestris scotia)* has a far greater claim to Scottishness. It's unique to the Scottish Highlands.

## RETURN OF THE NATIVE

What is a native British tree species anyway? There certainly aren't very many of them. When the last (or at any rate the latest) Ice Age finished about 12,000 years ago, there were no trees in Britain at all. The cold and the glaciers had wiped them all out. Between the time things warmed up enough for trees and the English Channel was formed about 6,000 years later, Britain was connected to Europe and trees were able to spread north. Only 30 or so species made it before the water closed behind them.

## BEATING ABOUT THE BUSH

I say '30 or so' because not everyone agrees which woody plants are big enough to count as trees and are not merely bushes or shrubs. Something woody that grows to 6 metres high is generally entitled to be called a tree. Though not the thing bananas grow on. A banana plant may look like a tree and be as tall as a tree and many people may call it a tree but, strictly speaking, it's just a herb with attitude.

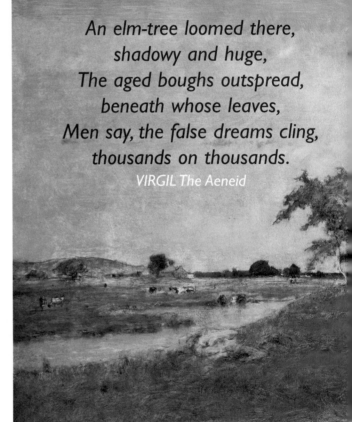

*An elm-tree loomed there, shadowy and huge, The aged boughs outspread, beneath whose leaves, Men say, the false dreams cling, thousands on thousands.*
VIRGIL *The Aeneid*

## BORN TO BE WILDWOOD

Are British woodlands made up of only about 30 tree species? Well, no. As in other parts of the world, the tree population has been much affected by humans – chopping them down in huge numbers but also taking and planting new species outside their natural range.

## GOING NATIVE

In Britain, many familiar trees thrive in local conditions once they've been given a helping hand to get here. They are not native but have *gone* native. Sycamores and Horse Chestnuts, for example, fall into this category. Human action in such cases has completed the distribution of trees otherwise prevented by accidents of geography.

## TREE MUSEUM

Trees of foreign origin have been cultivated in Britain for ages. Apple, cherry, pear – most fruit trees in our orchards were imported from other parts of the world. In our parks, estates and gardens there are dozens of types of trees not native to Britain. The London Plane, for example, is not a Londoner. It's a Spanish hybrid of the

## TRUE BRITS

*Many authorities have settled on 33 as the number of truly British native trees. They are: Alder, Ash, Aspen, Bay Willow, Beech, Bird Cherry, Black Poplar, Box, Common Oak, Crab Apple, Crack Willow, Downy Birch, Field Maple, Goat Willow, Hawthorn, Hazel, Holly, Hornbeam, Juniper, Large Leaved Lime, Midland Thorn, Rowan, Scots Pine, Sessile Oak, Silver Birch, Small Leaved Lime, Strawberry Tree, White Willow, Whitebeam, Wild Cherry, Wild Service Tree, Wych Elm and Yew.*

Oriental and American Plane. But it thrives in polluted streets and may be the tree most often seen by British city dwellers.

## TREE FARMS
In the 20th century, vast areas of this country were planted with fast-growing conifers to produce industrial quantities of timber. Not usually aesthetically pleasing or adding much to biodiversity, such trees now probably outnumber native species in upland Britain.

## WHEN? WHO? WYCH?
Until recently, most experts believed the 'English Elm' arrived in Britain in Neolithic times, brought by migrant humans from Europe. But it's now thought it was the Romans who first planted them, some three thousand years later. This seems like a big margin of error, but ancient pollen

samples are difficult to analyse, being easily confused with those of the Wych Elm (Ulmus glabra), which is a native species.

## BACK TO NATURE
One of the greatest living experts on British trees, Oliver Rackham, always doubted the theory that Neolithic settlers brought the English Elm to England. No other examples of this sort of long-range tree planting are known until Roman times. According to recent Spanish research published in Nature, DNA evidence shows that elms planted by the Romans in Italian and Spanish vineyards (where they were used to support grape vines) are identical with the English Elm. When I contacted Dr Rackham to tell him this, I assumed he would be impressed. But no, he is sceptical of this theory as well. Even if the DNA is identical (which he doubts) it proves nothing. Spanish and Italian elms could equally well have been taken there from England. For that matter, he does not accept the notion that elms were used to provide support for vines. His view is that a prehistoric introduction of English Elms into England is very unlikely and, though the Romans may have been responsible, it's not yet proven.

## MY OLD DUTCH
However they got here, English Elms flourished in Britain until they were destroyed in their millions by Dutch Elm Disease in the 1970s. Once a defining characteristic of the English landscape, the mature English Elm is magnificent – a straight trunk supporting a series of domes like a giant pear with its fat end upwards. Even people who don't get out much are likely to have seen in them the landscapes of Constable. Not so long ago, it would have been hard to imagine an England without her elms. That is, until it all went pear-shaped.

## NIGHTMARE ON ELM STREET
Dutch Elm Disease is caused by fungus spread by beetles that live in the elms' bark. It killed 90% of England's English Elms, perhaps 25 million trees in total. The disease is not really Dutch either. Early in the 20th century, research on the disease was first carried out by Dutch scientists (most of them women) and the name stuck.

## NO SEX PLEASE WE'RE ENGLISH
What made Dutch Elm Disease so deadly is that the English Elm doesn't reproduce sexually. Maybe this is what makes it so English. English Elms almost never grow from seeds: they spread by suckering. This means that the trees are genetic carbon copies of each other, which makes them particularly vulnerable. If a tree is susceptible to an infection, all of its suckers are too. So there have been many earlier instances of fatal elm disease: in the 20th and 19th centuries, and way back to the Neolithic era, when elms all over Europe were apparently hit by a huge decline.

## TREES ARE US
There are still English Elms around. If you happen to be in New York there's a famous English Elm in Washington Square. It is known as the Hangman's Elm because executions used to take place there. Nearer to home, Brighton managed to keep Dutch Elm disease at bay and has a few left, and there are a few more in Edinburgh. But if you really want to see English Elms in all their glory you need to go to Australia. Geographical isolation and stringent quarantine regulations mean Dutch Elm disease never got there. There are estimated to be 70,000 mature English Elms in the State of Victoria alone. You can find still small English Elms in English hedges because the suckers keep growing back. But as soon as they grow tall enough, Dutch Elm Disease kills them all off again.

## THE END OF THE ENGLISH ELM
So there you have it. The English Elm is probably not English. Stone Age Europeans may have planted it, or the Romans, or possibly neither of them. Either way it was in England before the English. And now there are hardly any left. This is because of Dutch Elm Disease, which is not Dutch. Quite interesting. Or, at any rate, quite complicated.

### ELM FACTS
- Elm trees can live for 300 years.
- Elm wood keeps its strength even when permanently wet, so it was used for keels and bilge planks; cart wheels; naval blocks and pulleys; wheelbarrows and coffins. Before cast iron, hollowed elm trunks were used as water pipes.
- According to Giraldus Cambrensis (Gerald of Wales), writing in the 12th century, English longbows were made of yew, but Welsh bows of elm.
- There are approximately 40 species of non-English Elm. They are found throughout the Northern Hemisphere from Siberia to Indonesia and from Mexico to Japan. The greatest diversity is in China.
- 'Elm Street' is the 15th commonest road name in the US.
- In the US, the value of a mature elm for insurance purposes is US $2,500.
- The 7,700,000 elms in North American towns are worth over US $19 billion.
- The cooling effect of one elm tree is equivalent to five air-conditioning units.

# *Gainful* EMPLOYMENT

## Why Not Become Pope?

THERE WAS A TIME when every boy wanted to be a train driver or a coal miner, but these days there's a whole new world of possibilities open for a young lad with the right attitude towards hard work and an ambiguous attitude towards women.

My advice to chaps has always been 'aim high', so for those of you thinking of going into the Church isn't it about time you said to yourself, 'Could I be the next Pope?' And just look at the benefits! Your own state (with you as supreme autocratic ruler), a job for life, infallibility (terms and conditions apply) and free access to nuns (no touching). I know it all sounds rather daunting at first, doesn't it, but then being a professional clog dancer is no picnic either. In both cases it pays for a lad to sit down with a piece of paper and a nice sharp pencil and draw up a list of requirements to see if the cap fits.

*Mr J. D. 'Bo'sun' Pollard, MA (Cantab.)*

### *So what does it take to become Pope?*

#### *1. Sex:*
Traditionally Popes have been men, with the exception of Pope Joan who lived in the ninth century and was entirely fictional. According to the legend she gave birth during a papal procession which rather compromised her position. The crowd, full of righteous Christian indignation, then quite correctly beat her and her child to death. So this is strictly a game for boys!

#### *2. Sex:*
Although frowned upon in the modern Church, plenty of Popes have mired themselves in the loathsome but strangely compelling sins of the flesh. During the eleventh century, the almost complete control over the papacy held by a group of papal mothers, lovers and prostitutes led to the period becoming known as the 'pornocracy'. Your Greek master can explain this word to you.

#### *3. Age:*
You don't have to be old to be Pope – far from it. The Church needs spunky young men to inject some fresh blood into its age-old institutions. Benedict IX allegedly became Pope when just eleven although, as we have no idea when he was born, the calculation is perhaps a touch shaky. John XII was certainly only eighteen when he became Pope, although he only survived nine years before being murdered by the irate husband of one of his lovers (see *'Sex'* above).

#### *4. Life:*
The best Popes have all been alive, but this is not an absolute requirement. Pope Formosus was exhumed, dressed in his papal robes and tried for sins against the Church when he was very much dead. Then they threw him in the Tiber.

#### *5. Belief:*
Believing in God is at least a nominal requirement for the job, but frankly this can hold you back in your pursuit of worldly self-interest. Over a dozen Popes have been charged with Satanism, which demonstrates a sort of belief. John XXII believed in magic. Boniface VIII believed Christianity was an invented religion and that Mary was as much a virgin as his own mother. Benedict IX simply believed the papacy was a good way to make money, selling the job to his godfather for 650 kg of gold.

#### *6. Goodness:*
Goodness me, what a sweet thought! There's nothing in the job description that requires a Pope to be good. Alexander was a married, philandering, nepotistic murderer (and a Borgia to boot) and he still got the top job. The Anti-Pope John XXIII was a pirate.

*Now before we get too excited and start filling in application forms willy-nilly you probably have some questions.*

#### *Don't I need to be a cardinal?*
Mais non! Urban VII wasn't a cardinal, although his election did start the Western Schism. It does help, however, and it can be easier than it looks. Leo X was made a cardinal at just fourteen and Cesare Borgia at eighteen – by his father who happened to be Pope *(Thanks Dad!)*.

#### *Don't I need the other cardinals all to vote for me?*
Now there's no need for such negative talk. There are 185 cardinals, but Innocent VII was elected by just eight. This is less than the number of cardinals you need to collect for your Boy Scouts 'Divinity' badge.

#### *Don't I have to be celibate?*
Frankly you're too young to know what that means, but if you'd care to remove your hand from your trousers, young man, I'll explain. Whilst celibacy is supposedly de rigueur for Popes, discretion is just as good, although some Popes haven't really bothered with this either. At least thirteen Popes have had illegitimate children, not always before they became Pope. Some of these have also been accused of bestiality, incest, fornication, adultery and rape. John XII was said to have turned the Lateran basilica into a brothel.

### *So there we are.*

Has this inspired you to become Christ's only vicar on Earth? If so, it's time to put away beastly thoughts of self-abuse, put down your penis and pick up a pen to apply. But before you ask the current Pope to move over and make way for some young blood there's one last thing to check. Is he dead? Unless you want to become an Anti-Pope or can persuade the living Pope to resign (and why should he?), this is a requirement. Traditionally the way to tell is to ask the Cardinal Camerlengo to hit the previous incumbent three times on the head with a silver mallet whilst shouting his baptismal name. If he's just having a nap this should wake him up. If he's dead it probably won't.

*Good luck chaps – or should I say, 'Your Holiness'!!!*

NEXT WEEK – HOW TO BECOME A BANK ROBBER.

70% of adults in the UK have no meaningful savings.

When Liverpool's Ian Rush was signed to Juventus for a year and asked how he found living in Italy, he said it was 'like being in a foreign country'.

Around 210,000 people are reported missing in Britain every year.

According to a *Which?* survey in 2005, 93% of the nutritional information on food labels is inaccurate.

Delays on British railways in 2001 resulted in a total of 3,500 years of wasted time.

Many young people in the UK think that the Battle of Britain took place in 1066.

65% of British schoolchildren cannot name a single composer and 69% don't know what a cello is.

Britain is the windiest country in Europe.

The amount of road space in Britain has grown by 25% since 1950, but the number of cars has increased by 700%.

There are 3,600 static and 460 mobile libraries in Britain, between them holding about 87 million books.

There are 50,000 practitioners of alternative medicine in Britain and 12,000 faith healers, but only 30,000 doctors.

23% of Britain's wealth is owned by 1% of the population.

There are at least 280,000 heroin and crack addicts in Britain who between them cost the British taxpayer £19 billion a year.

Ministries of the British Government currently employ more than 25,000 public relations officers.

There are about 80,000 prostitutes working in the UK.

Royal Mail staff steal about 200,000 letters and parcels every year and deliver 22 million letters to dead people.

In the UK's 2001 Official Census, 390,000 people entered their religion as 'Jedi'.

82% of Britons are surprised by their bank balance at the end of the month.

# EIGHTH-CENTURY EXAMINATION

## QI 700 (JP)

*Welcome to the eighth century. Before taking up residence you are required to pass a 'Life in the Eighth Century Test' which shows you understand the basics of Anglo-Saxon citizenship. Before taking this test you should read the 'Life in Anglo-Saxon England: A Journey to Ceorldom' handbook available from your local ealdorman.*

**QUESTION 1**
Is the statement below TRUE or FALSE?
Children under 10 shouldn't be hanged.
☐ TRUE
☐ FALSE

**QUESTION 2**
Where does the King live?
☐ Westminster
☐ Winchester
☐ Wilton
☐ No fixed abode

**QUESTION 3**
Is the statement below TRUE or FALSE?
Women can own things.
☐ TRUE
☐ FALSE

**QUESTION 4**
What is the main disadvantage of becoming a monk?
☐ The bad haircut
☐ The lack of sex
☐ The early mornings
☐ Having to learn to read
☐ Being hacked to death by marauding Vikings

**QUESTION 5**
Which of these statements is correct?
☐ There's no time for poetry in our kin-based warrior society
☐ Hwæt! We Gardena in geardagum
   þeodcyninga þrym gefrunon
   hu ða æþelingas ellen fremedon

*Please tick boxes as appropriate*

**QUESTION 6**
Which of these are NOT kingdoms in the heptarchy?
☐ Wessex      ☐ Northumbria     ☐ Sussex
☐ Essex       ☐ Southumbria     ☐ Isle of Man
☐ East Anglia ☐ Mercia          ☐ Runnymede
☐ Ford Anglia ☐ Kent

**QUESTION 7**
The City of London is mainly inhabited by:
☐ Rapists and pillagers
☐ Bankers and property speculators
☐ Rats, vermin and other creepy-crawlies
☐ Ghouls and denizens of hell

**QUESTION 8**
Someone cuts off your finger in a fight. In retaliation you cut off two of his toes. Who is worse off?
☐ He is – he can barely walk
☐ I am – I'll never play the harp again
☐ I'd call it even-stevens

**QUESTION 9**
According to the laws of Wessex, fire is:
☐ A boon
☐ A beggar
☐ A thief
☐ A useful way of getting Vikings out of your house

**QUESTION 10**
Is the statement below TRUE or FALSE?
Life expectancy in the eighth century is shorter than under the Romans.
☐ TRUE
☐ FALSE

**THE ANSWERS**

**Q1** TRUE – Laws vary from kingdom to kingdom but generally children under 10 (12 in some areas) are not considered responsible in law.

**Q2** No fixed abode – Eighth-century kings are peripatetic. Although they have palaces (in the broadest sense) the lack of an efficient administration means they have constantly to travel around their kingdom to prevent it all falling apart.

**Q3** TRUE – Women are individuals under Saxon law – unlike under Norman law where they are the possessions of their husbands or fathers.

**Q4** Since their first appearance at Lindisfarne in 793, being hacked to death by Vikings is certainly the most depressing drawback to a life in holy orders. Early mornings, on the other hand, are a way of life in Anglo-Saxon society, as are bad haircuts. Learning to read is a rare privilege, so that's nothing to complain about, and recent scandals suggest there is still an opportunity for sex in at least some Saxon monasteries, particularly the mixed ones.

**Q5** 'Hwæt! We Gardena in geardagum, þeodcyninga þrym gefrunon, hu ða æþelingas ellen fremedon.' As these lovely opening lines from the epic poem *Beowulf* (probably written in the late eighth century) show, there is plenty of time in Anglo-Saxon England for poetry.

**Q6** Ford Anglia, Southumbria, Isle of Man and Runnymede are not kingdoms of the heptarchy.

**Q7** It's full of ghosts. Many of the old Roman cities of Britain lie in ruins and are a focus for superstitions. With little understanding of what once happened in them (and no need for them) they are left abandoned and considered to be the realm of spirits.

**Q8** Even-stevens it is. Anglo-Saxon laws work on a compensation basis. Every person and every part of a person has a value that must be paid if an individual is deprived of it. A Welsh slave's life is worth half as much as a Welsh peasant's, and a member of the King's household is worth ten times that. Every body part also has a value, and a finger is worth two toes. So you're quits.

**Q9** According to the laws of King Ine of Wessex (688–726), fire is a thief for it can burn down trees in a forest. The axe used to fell a tree is considered an 'informer', however, not a thief.

**Q10** FALSE – Despite everyone going on about what the Romans did for us, life expectancy has increased for ordinary people since the collapse of Roman rule.

**HOW DID YOU DO?**
**0–3** Are you a Viking by any chance?
**4–8** Perhaps you should try the eighteenth century.
**9–10** You've passed! Welcome to the eighth century. Pull up a parasitic infestation and join us at the mead bench.

# Matt's English Proverbs

*Everything must have a beginning*

*Help me to salt, help me to sorrow*

*He who lies down with dogs will rise with fleas*

*Happy is the country that has no history*

*Don't halloo 'til you're out of the wood*

*Keep a thing seven years and you'll find a use for it*

*It will all be the same a hundred years hence*

*Cards are the devil's books*

# My idea of exercise is a good, brisk sit. PHYLLIS DILLER
# E X E R C I S E
## EIGHTEEN EX-OLYMPIC EVENTS
## (AND THE YEARS IN WHICH THEY WERE INCLUDED)

### Club Swinging (1904, 1932)
At the 1932 Games during the Depression, unemployed American George Roth won gold. After being awarded his medal in front of 60,000 spectators, he walked out of the stadium in Los Angeles and hitchhiked home.

George Roth
hits the
road again

### Cricket (1900)
Great Britain (actually Devon & Somerset Wanderers CC) beat 'France' (a team from the British Embassy in Paris). The French team was almost entirely made up of Englishmen.

### Croquet (1900)
Held at the Paris Olympics, France won all the medals in all the categories, as only French competitors took part.

### Duelling (1906)
Contestants didn't shoot at each other but at dummies in frock coats with a bulls-eye embroidered on the chest.

### Golf (1900, 1904)
Golf has only been an Olympic sport twice for men, and only once for women (in 1900). The USA took 9 of the 12 medals. All the female medallists were American – including Margaret Abbott, the first woman to win an Olympic gold. In 1904, Canadian silver medallist George Lyon accepted his trophy after walking to the podium on his hands.

### Lacrosse (1904, 1908)
Lacrosse was only held twice and it was a men's event. The bronze medallists in 1904 were a team of Mohawk Indians whose members included Rain-in-Face, Snake Eater and Man Afraid Soap.

... and last but certainly not least...
... mr man afraid soap

1904
OLYMPICS

**I am pushing sixty. That is enough exercise for me.**
MARK TWAIN

## Long Jump for Horses (1900)

A horse called Extra Dry won the only example of this event at the Paris Olympics with a jump of 20 feet and a quarter of an inch. It was a pretty poor effort – 2.63 metres short of the current world record for humans.

## Motor Boating (1908)

The 1908 Games were meant to be in Rome, but the Italians panicked after the eruption of Mount Vesuvius and London stepped in at the last minute. Since it was their Games, they added Motor Boating to the list of events. This was a disaster. The speed of the boats rarely exceeded a pedestrian 19 mph; six of the nine races were cancelled due to bad weather; and the three that were held were too far off shore to be seen by anyone.

## Obstacle Race (1900)

Competitors had to climb over a pole, scramble over a row of boats then swim under another row of boats. No Olympic swimming events were held in a pool until 1908. Before that they were in the river Seine (1900), a lake in St Louis, USA (1904), and, in 1896, in the sea. Gold medallist Alfred Guttmann commented: 'My greatest struggle was against the towering 12-foot waves and the terribly cold water.'

## One-Handed Weightlifting (1896, 1904, 1906)

## Pigeon Shooting (1900)

The Pigeon Shooting event was the only time in Olympic history when animals were deliberately killed. The birds were released in front of the competitors and the winner was the one who shot the most.

## Polo (1900, 1908, 1920, 1924, 1936)

At the 1908 London Olympics, Britain won all three medals. Teams from Roehampton and Hurlingham came first and second, and Ireland (then still part of Great Britain) took the bronze. The captain of the Irish team was John Hardress Lloyd, the great-uncle of the producer of *QI*.

## Real Tennis (1900)

Although held at the Paris Olympics and billed under its French name of Jeu de Paume, the US and Britain took all the medals.

## Rope Climbing (1896, 1904, 1906, 1924, 1932)

The object of the event was to shin up to the top of a rope. At the 1896 Olympics, only two competitors managed it. Over the years, they kept changing the length of the rope to try to get it right.

## Solo Synchronised Swimming (1984, 1988)

This contradiction in terms was thrown out as an official event in 1992. Supporters argued that the swimming was 'synchronised' to the music rather than to the other people in the team, but to no avail.

## Tug-of-War (1900, 1904, 1906, 1908, 1912, 1920)

Tug-of-War first became an Olympic event in 500 BC. In 1908, all the medallists were British police teams. The City of London Police took gold, Liverpool Police silver and the Metropolitan Police bronze. The USA, who were beaten in moments, accused the British of cheating – claiming their spiked boots gave them an illegal advantage. The British offered a rematch in their socks... and still beat the Americans.

## Tumbling (1932)

Introduced by the US at the Los Angeles Games and won by an American, Rowland 'Flip' Wolfe, using his revolutionary back-flip with double twist.

## Underwater Swimming (1900)

Competitors were awarded two points for each metre swum, and one point for each second that they stayed under water.

**I believe that the Good Lord gave us a finite number of heartbeats and I'm damned if I'm going to use up mine running up and down a street.**
NEIL ARMSTRONG

# Arthur Smith's... Edinburgh

## The Insider's Guide to the Edinburgh Festival

HOW TO GET...

1. FREE ACCOMMODATION.

Hang around the streets two days before the Festival until you see a van disgorge some young people in identical T-shirts. Observe which flat they go into and report there an hour later with your bags saying you are the lighting technician for 'the other show' and it's all been arranged with Murray. You will be given a room (sharing with nine others).

2. INTO EVERY SHOW WITHOUT PAYING.

Write PRESS in large red letters on an old train ticket. Adopt a look of extreme self-importance as you present it.

3. MONEY FOR NOTHING.

Look for a miserable man in the Assembly Rooms bar. Be sympathetic and earnest until he gives you money to help publicise his failing show. Take cash and dump leaflets in a bin.

4. FAMOUS.

Identify the hot new comedian and proposition him after his show. Unless you are physically repulsive and smell he will say yes. Use your phone to take pictures and ring papers the next day. Suggested angle:

**FUNNY MAN'S FUNNY WILLY**

T.V. EXEC

*This could make a great show on Channel 4*

5. YOUR OWN TV SERIES.

During the Edinburgh Television Festival run naked into the George Hotel, shit on the bar and shout that you are the new Messiah.

## Embroidery Tips

Life's too short for embroidery

## Experimental Art Works

'Oil on canvas' (oil on canvas)

*The Moving Finger writes; and, having writ, Moves on: nor all your Piety nor Wit Shall lure it back to cancel half a Line, Nor all your Tears wash out a single wo*

40

"According to the philosopher Epictetus (AD 55–135)," piped young Stephen, "we have two ears and one mouth so that we can listen twice as much as we speak." "What?" said the man.

"I say," exclaimed Stephen, "this puts me in mind of Epimetheus who foolishly opened Pandora's Box, thus releasing all manner of evil on the human race. And an anteater's cock, apparently!"

"If you're trying to measure the circumference of the earth, or the tilt of its axis," called Stephen from the boat, "you're wasting your time! It's already been done by Eratosthenes of Cyrene (276–194 BC)!"

"Very little is known of Euclid's life," said Stephen urgently, "but he may have been a pupil of Plato in Athens. Though he was not the greatest mathematician Greece produced (compared to, say, Archimedes), his *Elements* is one of the most influential books in the history of the world. Have one – it's a cracking read!"

"The principal doctrines of Epicurus", suggested Stephen, "were (1) That the highest good is pleasure and (2) That the gods do not concern themselves at all with human behaviour." "Get off me before I break your arm," said Polkinghorne Minor.

"Good gracious!" whispered Stephen. "We've caught Erichthonius, fourth King of Athens, red-handed, right here under the tuck-shop, inventing the chariot!"

"Don't be a fool!" cried Stephen. "In the words of Euripides (480–406 BC), 'Whom the gods wish to destroy, they first make mad.'" "Wasn't he the author of 95 plays?" grunted the Mountie. "Wrong!" parried Stephen, brilliantly. "Four of them were almost certainly by Critias!"

From outside the gunroom, came a mysterious voice. "Epicharmus (540–450 BC)", it intoned, "is said to have added the letters theta (θ) and chi (χ) to the Greek alphabet, invented comedy and been the first to use plots in drama." "Who on earth could that be at this time of night?" muttered the Brigadier.

Dr Huby burst into the room, angrily balancing a book on his ear. "Give me the dates of Epiphanius, Bishop of Salamis!" he demanded. "Circa AD 315–403," said Stephen, without looking up.

"The ancient Greek philosopher Empedocles (490–430 BC) killed himself by jumping into a volcano," insinuated Stephen pointedly.

"Who's this poor devil?" enquired Lady Hore-Glossop. "Epimenides of Crete," said Stephen firmly, "one of the Seven Wise Men of Greece and the man who introduced the temple to the country. While tending his flocks one day, he fell asleep in a cave for 57 years and, after he woke up, lived to be 289."

"Will you shut the fuck up about ancient Greeks beginning with E, or I'm going to have to kill you," said the man disguised as Mount Elbrus, the highest mountain in Europe, known to the ancients as Strobilos, Greek for spinning-top, and the place where Prometheus was chained for stealing fire from the gods.

## SLIPPERY FROG

Ever wondered why you don't see many frogs in winter? That's because frogs melt away into slime in the autumn. Then, by what Pliny astutely describes as 'a hidden operation of nature', they magically turn back into frogs in the spring.

# PLINY the ELDER's
# WONDERS
## of the
# NATURAL WORLD

1,800 years before Darwin there lived a great naturalist known as Pliny the Elder. Pliny was responsible for *Naturalis Historia*, the first great encyclopaedia. Made up of a whopping 37 volumes, the contents section alone ran to 70 pages. Pliny spent many years compiling his definitive guide to natural history, and he claimed that his book contained some 20,000 'important facts'. However, some of his facts were more important, if not indeed more *factual* than others. Here is a small selection of Pliny's pearls of ancient wisdom.

## CRAFTY BEAVER

The male beaver has a drastic method of avoiding predators. Pliny explained that beavers gnaw off their own testicles in order to throw hunters off their scent.

## MANTICHORA

In Pliny's day African wild-life was a lot more diverse than it appears to be today. This is the *mantichora*, essentially a lion, but with the head of a man and a scorpion's tail.

Sadly these, along with *pegasi* (flying horses) and *catoblepas* (the mere sight of which turn a man to stone) are now extinct.

## GIANT INDIAN LOCUST

Next time you're in India look out for the giant locusts, which grow up to three feet in length. Rather than creating a nuisance, these monster insects were in fact rather useful. Pliny suggested that once their bodies had been dried out, their legs could be removed and used as saws.

## EARWIGS IN EARS

Pliny was of the opinion that earwigs were no more likely to crawl into your ear than any other insect. But he was mindful of the fact that no matter how remote, the possibility did remain. He therefore included a simple remedy in his book. If an earwig does crawl into your ear, ask a friend to spit into it. The earwig will then come out again.

## THE EFFECTS OF EATING RABBIT

Pliny was not a fool. He was a scholar and man of reason. For example, he was sceptical about the popular Roman belief that eating rabbits made you sexually attractive, pointing out that this was possibly a play on words ('lepos' meaning grace, and 'lepus' meaning a hare.) But Pliny deemed it such a strongly held belief that it could not be without *some* justification. So he qualified his final judgement. He said that eating rabbit would make you sexually attractive, but the effects would only last nine days at the most.

## PEST CONTROL

There were no insecticides in Roman times, so a good deal of ingenuity was called for when dealing with troublesome pests. In Egypt, making a sacrifice to the goddess Isis was the standard procedure for exterminating flies. Pliny's top tip for ridding an apple orchard of insects was typically unconventional, yet remarkably simple. All you had to do was find a woman who was menstruating, and ask her, no doubt very politely, to walk around the orchard stark naked.

Gaius Plinius Secundus, to give him his proper name, lived from 23 to 79 AD. As well as a prolific author Pliny was a military commander of some repute. In August 79 he was serving as *praefectus* of the Roman navy at Misenum when he witnessed the great eruption of Mount Vesuvius. Eager to get a better view, he set sail across the Bay of Naples towards the disaster and, alas, his consequent demise. Pliny is still remembered in vulcanology, where the term 'plinian' refers to a very violent eruption of a volcano in which columns of smoke and ash rise into the stratosphere.

## THE HEROIC ANTHIAE

Air is soluble in water, or so says Pliny. That is why fish are able to breath, smell and hear. Among the fish he describes is the *anthiae*, a public-spirited creature which rescues its companions from anglers by severing fishing lines with its fin.

## SNAKE BITES

Pliny recorded that the traditional cure for a bite from an adder was to press a pigeon's arse against the wound. If the pigeon died the treatment was obviously working, so you applied the arse of another pigeon, and so on, until the pigeons eventually stopped dying, at which point you were cured. If no pigeons were readily available, Pliny personally recommended tearing open a live swallow, and applying its innards to the bite.

## TOP DARTS

Porcupines can fire their quills! Although Pliny made no mention of their range, or their accuracy.

## HEAVY SLEEPERS

Pliny believed that humans were heavy sleepers - quite literally. He claimed that the human body became heavier when a person slept. Similarly, he calculated that when a person died they put on weight.

CD 7/07

# THE FUN-Es

'Eye of newt, wing of bat, E102 tartrazine...'

'Let's face it, buddy – you're never going to forget.'

'This was due back next week!'

'It's from Mr Cummings!'

'I have this awful feeling I'm going to evolve into
Liam Gallagher.'

Newman

# The Poetry of QI

**MALE ANGLER FISH** *by Stephen Fry*

Male angler fish truly are pathetic.
It must be the feeblest male in
Nature, six times smaller than the female.

When they find a mate,
They latch onto them with their
Teeth and immediately start to disappear.

Scales, bones, blood vessels, all merge
Into those of the female, and
After a week, all that's left are two tiny little testes,
Which leak sperm into the female.

There are some of these female angler fish
Going around with about eight testicles
Hanging off them.

Brilliant.
It's like an Essex disco.

**OBSCURITY** *by Ronni Ancona*

Did you know about the word 'obscurity' before it got famous?
How it was beaten by its adjective father,
And left on the doorstep abandoned by its mother
And then it was the only noun growing up in a house of verbs.

But the verbs, they're always going out doing lovely things,
Because they're *doing* words,
And poor old obscurity was stuck inside suffering from asthma.

And then after school,
After school it was surrounded by quotation marks,
It got beaten up terribly,
And then one day it entered into a reality TV show,
And it became very famous
And it was much in demand
And used to describe all the people that leave *Big Brother* house.

**DAVID BECKHAM LIVES IN CHINGFORD** *by Ronni Ancona*
*& Stephen Fry*

The Battle of Culloden is quite complicated,
Because it was basically an Italian fop with a Polish accent,
A bunch of Highlanders, some Irish,
A few French, fighting some Scottish lowlanders and
English, led by a fat German from Hanover.

There were the Campbells and the Rosses
And the Grants and the Gunns
And many of the lowland families.

There were more Scots there beating
Prince Charles, Edward Stuart,
Than there were English.

It's so weird that these national heroes
Are not from the place that they're supposed to be.

William Wallace was from Kenya. His mother was Masai.

Not really
But David Beckham is definitely from Chingford.

**THE TROUSER PEOPLE** *by Stephen Fry*

Appropriately enough, this book on Burma
Is called *The Trouser People*.

To give you a foretaste,
It quotes the diary of Sir George Scott –
The man who introduced football to Burma
In the 19th century:

*Stepped on something soft and wobbly.*
*Struck a match.*
*Found it was a dead Chinaman.*

Those were very much the days, weren't they?
You wonder why the British are hated around the globe.

**HONEY** *by Alan Davies*

Eddie Izzard once observed,
It was very odd that bees make honey.
Earwigs, he said, don't make chutney.

It takes twelve bees an
Entire lifetime to make enough honey
To fill a teaspoon.

So the lifetime of twelve bees,
And you go into a
Supermarket and you see all those jars.

Think how many
Bees have been working away?
If it's a 125 ml jar,
It'll take three hundred bees.

**I HAD WIND WHEN I MET THE QUEEN** *by Julian Clary*

It was just a little smidge, as I thought.
And I tried to get rid of it
By internal squeezing, as can be done.

But it wasn't going to go –
So I thought, Well:
I'll discreetly let it go.

But unfortunately
On that occasion
I shat myself.

**OMNIPOD** *by Mark Steel*

The South Africans once picked,
For their cricket team,
A one-legged Norwegian.

And it was in the time of apartheid,
So it was, you know, quite poignant,
Because you were more likely to get
In the South African cricket team
If you were a one-legged Norwegian,
Than if you were black
With two legs.

*\*Euterpe, Greek for 'delight', is the Greek Muse of lyric poetry,*
*music and rejoicing.*

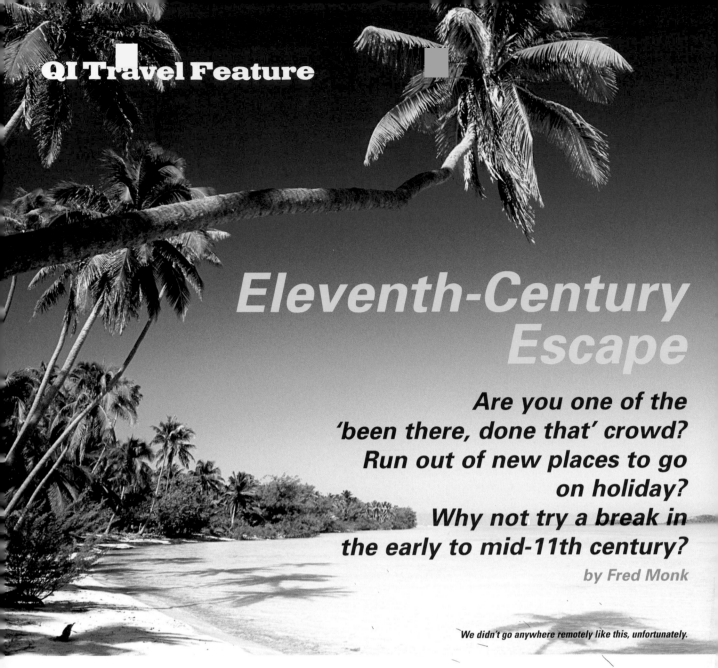

# Eleventh-Century Escape

### Are you one of the 'been there, done that' crowd? Run out of new places to go on holiday? Why not try a break in the early to mid-11th century?

*by Fred Monk*

*We didn't go anywhere remotely like this, unfortunately.*

**In these days when it seems almost impossible to find a genuinely 'new' travel destination, perhaps it's time we stopped thinking about 'where' and started thinking about 'when'?**

I don't think the kids (or their mum Jocasta for that matter) were convinced when I said that we were going to try an 11th-century mini-break, which my wife described as sounding like 'Butlins with typhoid'. But without even so much as an **au pair** in tow we packed our bags and headed off **en famille.**

We arrived in 1002, just in time to witness King Ethelred's massacre of the Danish population of England – which certainly proved to us that he wasn't as 'unready' as the history books make out! Our hovel was built out of local materials (mud and sticks) and blended beautifully with its environment (a mire). In these days before large-scale stone building, it's good to see regionally sourced, environmentally friendly style is back in fashion.

There was a simple open fire in the middle of the room (no stuffy old chimneys here!) set on a beaten earth floor. Decoration consisted of a handloom in the corner (used to make the lively local textiles, often depicting battles), some authentic flint-tempered pottery and a wooden bench and table. A single small window enhanced the atmospheric gloom, and someone had thoughtfully stretched a piece of oiled cloth across it. That, and the choking smoke from the fire, ensured that any light that might have seeped in was most unlikely to blind us.

The locals seem to go in for 'studio living', and we found the sleeping area in the same room. The beds consisted of a lavish pile of animal skins and sacks of hay. If I had a complaint it would be with the laundry department as these were generously supplied with lice, which we'll be picking from the children's hair for months. The slave offered to drape our bedding over the cesspit so that the rising ammonia would kill the bugs, but Jocasta didn't like the idea of her bed smelling of wee-wee so we declined. We were also initially surprised to find that a number of other guests, including a cow and two goats, were sharing with us. We were firmly told that this was not a booking error but, being winter, animals are brought in both to protect them from the cold and to help to keep the human inhabitants warm.

The food, to be honest, took a little getting used to. On the plus side, it's fresh – apart from the smoked meats – homemade, seasonal and organic. On the minus side, it's relentlessly disgusting. We'd opted for the 'peasant food' package after a wonderful holiday on a Tuscan olive farm last year but this was frankly a long way from **cucina di campagna**. The main meal, eaten off stout wooden platters, was a thin stew of local vegetables ('weeds' Jocasta called them, and not without reason) livened up with some grain, a lot of grit and the merest hint of a piece of pork (meat apparently being rather expensive). The children were, not surprisingly, furious that chips hadn't been invented yet. This was all washed down with small ale (for the kids!) and a stronger brew for the grown-ups, although neither was bitter – hops not reaching England for another 600 years. Drinking the local water unboiled is frowned upon – mainly because this can prove fatal.

As with any family holiday, the first thing on our minds, after an initial, crippling bout of dysentery, was finding things to do. Coming from an age of theme parks and Playstations, what could the 11th century offer a kite-surfing, off-roading, seen-it-all modern family? Well, provided you like singing, drinking and casual violence – quite a lot! The Danish invasion of 1009 (repeated 1013) showed that the English are by no means the worst behaved tourists. The Danes, who arrived by boat after what was clearly a rather rough crossing, not only hogged the best seats but proved to be savagely brutal, subjugating the whole nation to their will. But as Jocasta pointed out, at least the furniture and bathing habits might improve.

The highlight, for the kids at least, had to be the battle of Hastings in 1066. These were the days when people had to make their own entertainment, and they put on a show as though their lives depended on it – which, of course, they did. Watching 15,000 exhausted men cutting each other to pieces for hour upon hour on Senlac Hill was a treat, although we'd have liked a sniff of some toilet facilities. I won't spoil it for you, but do make sure you stay for the last stand of Harold II's housecarls as they gather around him to fight to the death with their long-handled axes – pure cinema!

In the evenings, things quietened down a bit and, whilst the wounded were patched up using folk remedies from what they colourfully call 'leechbooks', the rest of us clustered around the fire for an evening of singing and spectacularly heavy drinking. Once a week, a local 'scop' or bard visits the hovel, his shout of 'Hwæt!' signalling the beginning of one of his Germanic stories, poems or songs. Jocasta found the epic poetry rather moving, although the kids got a bit bored. They livened up (as did I) when the obscene riddles started. My favourite began, **'I stand erect in a bed.'** Can you guess what I am?

As the sun dips and its last rays struggle to get past the oilcloth and the acrid fumes from the fire and the cow, the heady atmosphere and pints of mead begin to take their toll. Most of the locals fall comatose where they are, but we stagger off to our lousy beds for some well-earned rest. Tomorrow will start at dawn (they're all early birds here!) when our new local Norman lord has offered to 'harry' us. We'll have to wait until tomorrow to find out exactly what that means.

## GETTING THERE

It takes over 1,000 years to get from the beginning of the 11th century to the present day. Travelling back to the 11th century is frankly impossible for a number of temporal and philosophical reasons. We pretended.

## WHERE TO STAY

The accommodation in the 11th century varies from rude 'huts' (like the hovel we stayed in) to impressive wooden 'halls' – usually the homes of the aristocracy. There are almost no stone buildings, with the exception of a handful of churches, until after the Norman Conquest. Even then the early Norman castles are impressive on the outside but hardly comfortable.

## WHAT TO TAKE

A good medical kit – although there are a number of sophisticated herbal remedies available, they won't really help with the endemic typhus, cholera (in built-up areas – not that there are many of these) and tuberculosis. Do take water-purifying tablets to avoid throwing up at both ends or stick to the mead and ale which is boiled during manufacture and hence sterile (-ish). Polio, diphtheria and smallpox are also common, as is the occasional outbreak of bubonic plague, so it's best to check with your doctor about vaccinations before you leave.

## WHAT TO BRING BACK

There are a number of good-value craft items available, although some are a little 'rustic'. Look out for Stamford ware pottery with its lurid yellowy-green glaze, the colour of stale urine. Weapons are good value, especially the local single-bladed knife or 'scramseax'. Everyone here carries weapons, although you'll get into trouble if you draw a sword in the King's hall. Handmade textiles are plentiful although remember what is often called a 'tapestry' is actually an embroidered cloth – William the Conqueror got this wrong. Ultimately, the 11th century is an unspoilt, pre-industrial world. The real traveller brings home only memories (and perhaps tapeworm).

*An artist's impression of our hovel*

# The epistles we get - a dip into the QI mailbag...

Dear Sir,

In your last show, Stephen Fry Esq. confidently told the British public that the male iguana possessed two 'penises'. Not so!

Many years ago, I found myself in the happy situation of being posted with the British Army in the Amazonian rainforest. (Trouble with the natives!) I remember those days fondly. Pink gins on the veranda, pygmy hunts on Thursdays and a charming batman called Tufty. But I digress. As it so happens, our battalion kept a pet iguana. Fine fellow called Spartacus. Bit of a gammy leg, but he entertained the chaps for hours. Anyway, I distinctly remember that Spartacus had three cocks, not two. Splendid things they were. He was always showing them off to the gals.

Anyway, just thought you should know!

Pip, pip and keep up the good work.

Yours faithfully, Major Giles H. Ferguson, The Wirral


Dear Mr Alan Davies Sir,

May I call you Alan? Greetings! It is your friend Amobi Abachai from Nigeria. You must be remembering me as I emailed you chain letter and you then placed £1,500 in my offshore bank account for your share in the moneys left behind by my father, the late General Sani Abachai.

You may remember that my father, bless his soul in heaven glory glory hallelujah, was most regrettably ousted in the recent coup by Chief Olusegun Obasanjo. Although I promised you that you would get 10% of my father's $565 Million US Dollars inheritance fund, I must regrettably inform you that matters have become difficult for me in Nigeria. Chief Olusegun Obasanjo has captured me and put me in a very deep snake pit with only a packet of Kellogg Pop Tarts to keep me alive, and my wireless laptop to keep my sanity mind. As such, I am needing to commandeer a military force to help me escape and need to recruit British SAS. Please help my escape by placing £150,000 into my usual account BANK OF NIGERIA: 345454366, SORT: 349234. Thanking you!

Your friendship forever,

Amobi Abachai (P.S. Your money come soon!)


Dear Sirs,

I think I could help you get a bigger audience for your show. By implying that QI is only Quite Interesting, I am sure you are missing out on a lot of people who would want to watch a Very Interesting programme. In my last job (in politics), I had similar success by changing the name of a party from 'Labour' to 'New Labour'. Hey, presto! Everyone was fooled into thinking they were going to get a different kind of political party. For a mere £1.5 million (and a book deal afterwards), the advice is yours to keep.

All the best,

Alastair Campbell, Hôtel Enorme, Cap d'Antibes

(P.S. Or what about Amazingly Interesting?)


Dear Mr Titchmarsh,

Surely begonias bloom in shady spots during the summer and not the other way round?

Love, your admirer,

Sally Frimbly, Surrey (P.S. Knickers enclosed)


Dear Sir,

I recently chanced upon the Christmas episode of your television programme, IQ. Quite frankly, it wasn't a patch on Ant and Dec's Saturday Night Takeaway and Animals Do the Craziest Things but worse still you are grievously misinformed about the festive arrangements at Sandringham. You were, I grant you, correct in saying that members of the Royal Family open their gifts on Christmas Eve (a German tradition) and that Her Majesty drinks her own blend of Indian Tea. However, it is simply not true to suggest that the Queen's favourite presents of all time were 'a casserole dish and a gift-wrapped washing-up apron'. That is a damned lie, and you know it. This is just what we have come to expect of the bearded homosexual Communists and fellow travellers who run the BBC! By far the Queen's favourite Christmas present was when Andrew dumped Fergie.

Get your bloody facts straight!

Yours faithfully,

Philip, HRH The Duke of Edinburgh


Dear Sir,

Ahoy there!

As the founder of Anagram Weekly Magazine, I wondered whether you realised what a treasure trove of fun you can have with the name of your resident panellist, Alan Davies?! It occurred to me that Alan would drive 'a ladies van' on his way to the shopping centre to do 'a vandalise'. As a well-known pigeon fancier, he could go to the pet shop to pick up some 'avian leads' by paying on 'a laden Visa', or go to the doctor for 'a nasal dive', some 'anal advise' and 'a saved nail'.

If he was peckish and had 'a saliva den', I'd imagine he'd go and buy 'a salad vine'. Only a thought!

Yours,

Dean Vialas


Dear Stephen Fry,

Hi! I'm from Ukraine and I would like to meet kind man to be my guide and maybe more. So if you haven't wife or girlfriend now, you may reply please. I'm going to work in UK for five months. My friends tell I look well enough. Please send your letter directly to my email mary.svetlana@ukraimail.com and I send my foto to you. I am waiting for your reply.

Buy,

your Mary, Ukraine

# East
## ROGER LAW'S CHINA

MAO IS FUCKING WONDERFUL

**Above:** Jingdezhen, or 'Porcelain City', has a population of one and a half million, all of whom are involved in the manufacture of China's much coveted porcelain. Even today, some of these ceramics are worth more than their weight in gold.

**Right:** In Jingdezhen, even the lamp posts are made of porcelain. Each street has its own distinct design – peach blossom, dragons etc.

**Below:** The word porcellana derives from the Latin porcus, which means both 'pig' and 'pudendum' and is where the word 'pork' comes from. Cowrie shells are supposed to look like a sow's fanny.

**Left:** In Chinese, Qin is pronounced 'Chin', which is how it used to be spelt in English. Although the Qin dynasty lasted only 15 years (221–206 BC), this is where the word 'China' comes from – both the country and the stuff that plates are made from. China was called 'china' or 'china ware' in English because of its country of origin.

**Right:** McDonalds in China is known as 'The American Embassy'

**Above:** Each month, five million more Chinese acquire a mobile phone. The reception is often better in remote parts of China than it is in Norfolk. Many beauty spots (such as Guilin's famous limestone mountains) sport masts and barefoot peasants can be seen ploughing with oxen whilst yelling into their mobiles.

**Below:** In Mandarin, the word 'secretary' and 'honey' have the same pronunciation, and 'sweet honey' has the same sound as 'little secretary'. In President Jiang Zemin's new China, a 'little secretary' is an essential status symbol.

**Above:** The current slang for 'gay' in the new capitalist China is 'comrade'

**Above:** Nappies are not used in rural China. Instead, babies and toddlers have no seams in their trouser seats, allowing a quick-release action for number ones and twos.

**Left:** The Chinese barber or hairdresser is often a knocking shop. The Chinese character for 'leisure' also means 'brothel'. Under Mao, most towns and cities had a 'People's Square'. These have now been renamed 'Leisure Square'.

**Right:** The demonstrations and subsequent killings in Tiananmen Square are now referred to as 'The Accident'.

**Above:** Who killed cock sparrow? There are very few sparrows in China. Mao decreed that every family in China had to kill one a week to stop them eating all the rice. Sparrows do not eat rice.

**Above:** Mao awoke one morning and, in his wisdom, decreed that every Chinese family should present a set number of rats' tails to Communist officials each week. Unlike the sparrow campaign, the rats proved more elusive. Families found the solution by breeding rats to make up their quota of tails.

**Above:** Mao is the patron saint of Chinese taxi drivers. The Chinese have a popular urban myth that when Mao died, he descended into hell – whereupon Old Nick put him in charge of the traffic department.

**Left:** There is no such thing as a comfortable chair in the whole of China.

# eyes

The vast majority of people entering a shop look left and turn right. Thereafter, women look down and men look up. Products placed 3–4 feet above the floor have the greatest overall sale potential, but exotic high-priced foods are placed on the higher shelves because very few women buy them.

The word 'pupil' is from the Latin *pupillus*, a little child or doll – after the tiny reflection of yourself you see when you look into someone else's eye. The same concept exists in all Indo-European languages as well as Swahili, Lapp, Chinese and Samoan. The ancient English word for pupil was 'eye-baby'.

Eyelash mites are tiny creatures with eight stumpy legs and wormlike bodies that live in the base of the eyelashes, as many as 25 to a follicle. They are so efficient at processing the dead skin they eat that they don't have an asshole.

*Two men lay claim to the invention of false eyelashes. The first is Max Factor (1887–1938), who also invented the eyebrow pencil, lip-gloss and 'pancake' make-up, and was the first person to sell cosmetics for non-theatrical use. He started his career as an apprentice dentist in Poland. The other is the film director D. W. Griffith (1875–1948), who also invented the crane shot. His false eyelashes were made for Seena Owen who played Princess Beloved in the movie* Intolerance *(1916). They were so cumbersome that she could only wear them a few hours at a time before her eyes swelled up and closed.*

About 15 babies in the UK each year are born without eyes, a horrific condition known as anopthalmia.

Only one creature on earth is normally born with one eye, a primitive fish called the Cyclops. Most insects have five eyes. The word senocular means 'having six eyes'. Most spiders have eight eyes. Grasshoppers have ten eyes. Caterpillars have 12 eyes, though the butterflies they turn into have only four.

According to former French president François Mitterrand, Mrs Thatcher has 'eyes like Caligula and the mouth of Marilyn Monroe'.

Luis Buñuel's Surrealist movie *Un Chien Andalou* (1929) featured a number of dead donkeys provided by Salvador Dali. He laid them out on grand pianos and cut out their eyes with a pair of scissors.

On July 16th 1945, the physicist Richard Feynmann was the only person to see the explosion of the first atomic bomb with the naked eye. Knowing that bright light alone can't harm the human eye, he refused to wear the regulation-issue dark glasses and watched it through the windscreen of a truck, which was sufficient to shield his eyes from harmful ultraviolet radiation.

'THE EYE OF GOD'

*Left: The Helix Nebula is 650 light years away in the constellation of Aquarius.*

In 1210, after a three-day siege of the town of Bram, Simon de Montfort seized the garrison. He cut off the noses and upper lips of more than 100 men and gouged their eyes out. Just one man was left with a single eye and ordered to lead his blind comrades to safety at the next town. De Montfort's strategy was to panic those defending the chateau at Cabaret into surrender as they saw coming down the road a party of living skulls, complete with grinning teeth and a triangular gap in the centre of the head topped by sightless eyes. This appears to us the act of a heartless monster, yet all those who knew de Montfort described him as handsome, charming, saintly, pious, noble, etc. Whatever his supposed charms and brilliant military strategy, de Montfort failed to capture Cabaret (HURRAH!), which eventually surrendered over a month later under diplomatic rather than military pressure.

*I have eyes like those of a dead pig.*
MARLON BRANDO

The human eye can take in a million simultaneous impressions and tell the difference between 8 million different colours. On a clear, moonless night the human eye can detect a match being struck 50 miles away.

An 'eye-servant' is someone who can only be trusted to do any work when his or her employer is watching.

*The eyes are the spoons of speech.* ARABIC PROVERB

Dante Gabriel Rossetti (1828–1882) had such bad eyesight that he wore two pairs of spectacles on top of each other.

The eyes of a buzzard are five times sharper than a human's. A person with exceptional eyesight may just be able to make out a rabbit flicking its ears from 100 yards away. A buzzard can do so from a distance of 2 miles.

11% of guide dogs in New Zealand are short-sighted. The eyesight of some of them is so poor that, if they were human, they would have to wear glasses.

Apart from the head chef, everyone who works at the Blindekuh ('Blind Cow') Restaurant in Zurich is either blind or partially sighted. Meals are served in pitch darkness, so that, in a reverse of the norm, sighted customers are entirely reliant on the help of the blind waiters and waitresses.

The philosopher René Descartes (1596–1650) had a fetish for cross-eyed women. He conquered this when he realised that the root of his fascination was a little girl with cross-eyes whom he had played with as a child. He used this insight to support his belief that human beings have free will.

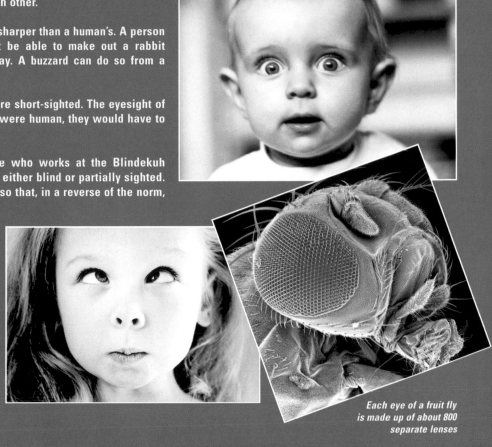

*Each eye of a fruit fly is made up of about 800 separate lenses*

# WHOSE EYE IS THIS?

A: Meerkat  B :Swan  C: Human  D: Seal  E: Lion  F: Seagull  G: Dragonfly  H: Cow  I: Elephant  J: Pelican  K: Eagle Owl  L: Ostrich

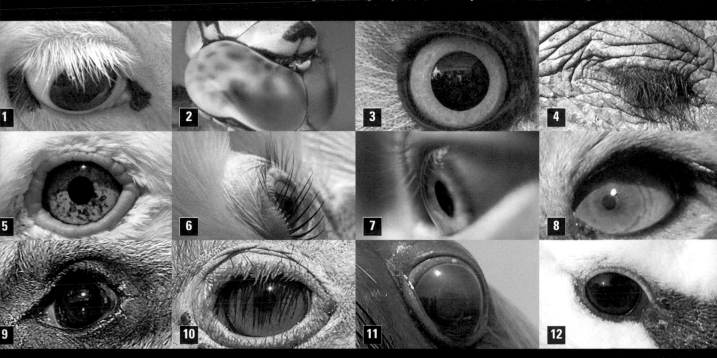

ANSWERS – 1: Cow. 2: Dragonfly. 3: Eagle owl. 4: Elephant. 5: Seagull. 6: Seagull. 7: Pelican. 8: Human. 9: Lion. 10: Meerkat. 11: Seal. 12: Swan.

This is not Sir James Jeans

# ears

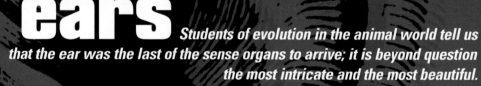

*Students of evolution in the animal world tell us that the ear was the last of the sense organs to arrive; it is beyond question the most intricate and the most beautiful.*
**SIR JAMES JEANS (1887–1946)** *Science and Music*

The ancient Chinese believed that the ears indicated character and destiny. Long earlobes meant long life, thick ones wealth. They also believed that the longer a person's ears, the nobler he would be. Kings and emperors of Old China all supposedly had extremely long ears (as do all statues of Buddha). The ears of Liu Bei, founder of the Han dynasty in AD 221, are said to have reached his shoulders. He could see his own ears just by glancing round.

*For women the best aphrodisiacs are words. The G-spot is in the ears. He who looks for it below there is wasting his time.*
**ISABEL ALLENDE**

This woman is not an ancient Chinese. She's from Sarawak in Malaysia.

The smallest muscle and the smallest bone in the human body are in the ears. The smallest muscle is the *stapedius,* which is just over 1 mm long.  Paralysis of this results in a condition called *hyperacusis,* which causes normal sounds to seem extremely loud. The second smallest muscle in the body is also in the ear. It's called the *tensor tympani* and is used to reduce the noise caused by chewing. The smallest bone is the stirrup bone. It's between 2 mm and 3 mm long and is shaped just like a tiny stirrup. It is also known as the *stapes,* from the mediaeval Latin for stirrup, *stapeda* or *stapedium* – literally 'foot-stand'. This is a made up word dating from the 14th century. There was no such word in classical Latin. Stirrups were unknown to the ancient Romans. They were a Chinese invention, dating from around the time of Christ. Later, they reached India, where the aristocracy both walked and rode barefoot. An Indian stirrup was originally just a ring for each big toe. Without stirrups, it is impossible to fight on horseback. Some historians believe that the adoption of stirrups by the cavalry of the Frankish King Charles Martel in AD 732 enabled the creation of the feudal system.

*It is all very well to be able to write books, but can you waggle your ears?*
**J. M. BARRIE (1860–1937)**

An okapi can wash its own ears inside and out with its tongue. Crickets have their ears on their forelegs. A cicada's ears are on its stomach. The praying mantis has only one ear, located in the centre of its chest.

Spiders do not have ears at all. They hear with minuscule hairs on their legs. This is not as strange as it sounds. Human hearing works the same way. Inside each human inner ear are approximately 15,000 extremely sensitive little hairs. These enable us to hear a whisper from many feet away, but loud noises (such as rock music or firing a shotgun without ear defenders) gradually destroy the hair cells. If you are standing next to someone and you have to shout to make yourself heard, you can be sure that the noise is damaging your ears. The hair cells in the ears are irreplaceable, and the loss of them is one of the principal causes of deafness. Human hearing starts to get gradually worse from the age of 20.

The inner ears of lobsters contain sand, which may explain why they can only hear things at very close range. Gravity keeps the sand at the bottom of their ears and tells the lobsters they're the right way up. Researchers replace the sand with iron filings. They use a magnet to move these around inside the lobster's head and fool it into flipping upside down. This greatly amuses the researchers.

The things that look like ears on an owl are tufts for display purposes only. Owls' ears are recessed into the sides of their faces, usually right at the outer edge of the ring of feathers around the eye. This feathery disc acts like a parabolic dish, focusing the sound waves into the ear canal entrance. The ears are positioned at different heights on each side of the head, enabling the owl to hear which vertical (as well as which horizontal) direction any sound may be coming from.

**EAR-BASED PARTY TRICK**
The oils and fats in earwax destroy the froth on beer by lowering the surface tension of the bubbles, which burst. People who wear glasses can get the same effect by using the sweat that collects on the bridge of the nose. Even the smallest traces of fat have this effect, but western earwax works better than oriental; most Asians have dry earwax, with a lower fat content.

John Bennet, aged 36, a Londoner, was today ordered to seek treatment at a psychiatric hospital after biting off the ear of a Danish Labour Exchange Official. Mr Bennet, from Hendon, who has lived for four years in Denmark, was found guilty of knocking down the official and chewing off his ear when he was refused public funds to go to Norway to look for a job. The local court was told that when the official recovered consciousness after the attack, he found his ear on a desk with a note that read 'Your Ear'. **THE TIMES**

# Excommunication Exclusive!

**Q1** is proud to present the first extracts from the recently discovered (unauthorised) Calendar of Saints featuring the Merry Month of May, by Frederick the Monk

**3rd May** St James The Lesser is perhaps not a title you'd aspire to but, as a cousin of Jesus, he certainly had a few stories to tell. The two most famous are that he prayed so frequently that the skin on his knees thickened until it looked like a camel's and that, after the crucifixion, he vowed to fast until Jesus returned. Jesus promptly then not only appeared unto James but also rustled up a spot of lunch for him. He was eventually martyred by being thrown from a tower of the temple in Jerusalem and then beaten to death with sticks.

**4th May** A day for firefighters to raise a glass to their patron, St Florian, an officer in the Roman army who is said to have put out a fire in the town of Noricum in modern-day Austria using a single bucket of water. This could be considered miraculous, or alternatively he might have overstated the scale of the fire.

**6th May** St Evodius was traditionally one of the 72 disciples commissioned by Jesus. He was ordained by St Peter and became Bishop of Antioch. What is quite interesting about him is that he's the first person on record to use the term 'Christian'.

**8th May** St Gibrian didn't do anything too miraculous but he came from a really wonderfully pious family – his siblings included St Tressan, St Helan, St Germanus, St Abran, St Petran, St France, St Promptia, and St Possenna. Just imagine what fun Sunday lunch must have been!

**10th May** St Simon the Apostle has to make any list of cruel and unusual martyrdoms, having been sawn in half. And it wasn't a trick.

**11th May** St Gengulphus, tiring of his wife's numerous affairs but not wishing to embarrass her publicly, retired to a hermitage in his castle at Avallon. One would have thought that his wife and her lovers would have been delighted that they could now get on with whatever they fancied without Gengulphus breathing down their necks, but no, one of the lovers tracked the poor old chap down and murdered him in his bed.

**12th May** Move right down the platform... it's St Pancras' day! St Pancras was an orphan brought by his uncle St Dionysius to Rome where he promptly converted to Christianity and was just as promptly martyred, aged only 14. Some 350 years later, Pope Vitalian had the wizard idea of digging him up and sending his remains to England, where the natives were proving unwilling to convert. St Pancras was duly shipped off to a delighted St Augustine of Canterbury, who'd only recently got his feet under the Archbishop and Primate of All England's desk. He split up the remains and immediately went about installing them in the altars of all the new churches he was busy building, each of which he dedicated to the saint.

**13th May** St Imelda Lambertini was a student at a Dominican convent who showed particular dedication to St Agnes, to whom she frequently prayed. As a reward for this she received her first communion 'miraculously' when aged only 11 and then promptly died in an ecstasy of love and joy.

**15th May** We should perhaps say 'Hats Off' – or, considering the form of his martyrdom 'Heads Off!' – to St Boniface of Tarsus, who had the pleasure of being converted by a Roman matron with the unusual name of Algae. And let's not forget St Matthias the Apostle, the patron saint of alcoholism.

**16th May** On May 10th 1657, St Andrew Bobola was living in Pinsk in Russia trying to persuade Russian Orthodox Christians to convert to Catholicism when Cossacks raided the city. Cossacks weren't all that fond of Jesuits, so when they caught him they first beat him, then tied him to a horse and dragged him through the streets. They then attacked him with knives, skinned him alive and finally beheaded him, just to be sure.

**18th May** St Felix of Cantalice was not necessarily someone you'd want to invite to a dinner party or any other social gathering. His great trick was that he could 'see' your sins – an ability so disconcerting that sinners used to hide from him in the street. A man of great piety, his funeral was so well attended that a hole had to be knocked in the church wall to get all the mourners out after the service without being crushed.

**19th May** St Calocerus was a eunuch made Governor of Anatolia by the Roman emperor Decius. When Decius accused him of the twin crimes of embezzlement and Christianity, Calocerus chose to defend Christianity. One can only assume this meant he felt he didn't stand a chance on the embezzlement rap. Sadly he was convicted on both counts and Decius ordered him burnt alive. As is often the way with saints, however, the flames refused to burn him, so his guards had to beat him to death with the fiery brands.

**20th May** This is a good day for advertisers, public relations personnel and compulsive gamblers (all of which amounts to roughly the same thing), as it's their patron's day. St Bernadino of Siena made his name as one of the most charismatic of all medieval preachers, enlivening his act with bonfires of the vanities, collective weeping (always fun) and exorcisms – a sort of righteous Paul Daniels. The Blessed Columba of Rieti also knew some neat tricks. She was prone to mystical out-of-body ecstasies, in one of which she toured the Holy Land, thus saving her the time and inconvenience of having to visit in person.

**21st May** St Godric wrote the song 'Sainte Nicholaes', the earliest surviving piece of lyric poetry in English. He was a serious ascetic living in Finchale, Co. Durham, in a mud hut. To make this even more miserable he insisted on going barefoot, wearing a hair shirt (under a metal breastplate just to make sure it rubbed), living only off gathered fruits and berries and standing in a bucket of icy water to control his lust. To his further satisfaction, no doubt, Scottish raiders repeatedly arrived to beat him up, under the inexplicable impression that he had some buried treasure lying about. 'Look! – there's a bloke in a hut wearing a hair shirt and standing in a bucket of water. He must be rich – let's mug him.'

**23rd May** St William of Rochester was not actually from Rochester, he was from Perth in Scotland. However, he did go to Rochester, which is rarely a wise move. A bit of a wild child before he had a sudden conversion to Christianity and decided to become a baker, for a while he lived a good and simple life baking bread, giving one in 10 of his loaves to the poor and attending Mass each day. Then one day he was on his way home from Mass when he found an abandoned baby on his doorstep. Being a lovely man, he took the lad in, called him David and brought him up as his own – even teaching him the baking game. Everything was going swimmingly until William suggested to David that they should go on a pilgrimage to the Holy Land. After making a suitably large supply of professionally turned-out sandwiches for the trip, the two headed off. They had only got as far as Rochester when it all went a bit wrong. For some reason (hormones??) David turned on William and hit him with a club. He then cut his throat and stole his money and ran away. Fortunately, there was a happy ending. An insane old woman found William's body, put a garland of honeysuckle on it and was promptly cured of her madness. Some monks who had been watching this got very excited. It just so happened that they were looking for a saint to put in their cathedral in Rochester to cash in on the pilgrimage trade (or to 'venerate' as they liked to put it) – and there right in front of them was a bona fide miracle! So everyone went home happy. Except St William, of course.

**24th May** Things started going wrong for St Simon Stylites the Younger with his father's death, when he was just 5 years old. Thankfully, a kindly monk took Simon in, but it soon turned out he was a sociopath, and, when Simon was 7, he suggested they both move to the top of pillars to get a bit of peace and quiet. The plan didn't quite work out as expected as, once everyone heard there were two blokes living on pillars, they naturally wanted to throng to them. The two unlucky hermits had to keep building their pillars up to get away from the crowds. Starting at a perfectly sensible dwelling height of

3 feet, after 13 years they were 60 feet up in the air. At this point, Simon climbed down his pillar and hid in the mountains to get away from everyone and particularly from the kindly monk whose rotten idea it was. Eventually, a group of would-be students tracked him down and persuaded him to start a monastery for them. This he did, placing at its centre a brand new pillar for him to live on. He was then ordained a priest, which was rather tricky for the bishop doing the ordaining. Simon wouldn't come down, so the bishop had to go up. This made things even more difficult for the monks, as every time they wanted their new priest to celebrate communion they had to fetch a ladder. St Simon died up there at the ripe old age of 76. Of those 76 years he had spent 69 on pillars.

**26th May** At the age of 10 St Mary Ann de Paredes decided to become a hermit, not in the traditional mud hut/cave etc. but in her sister's house, which must have made for some awkward moments at dinner parties. She chose to live entirely on consecrated wafers and communion wine, supplemented by one ounce of dry bread every 8 to 10 days. ('The Eucharist Diet' – it could well catch on!) After the 1645 earthquake in Quito, Ecuador (where she lived), there was (as so often happens after earthquakes) an epidemic, and Mary Ann decided to offer herself as a sacrifice to God to spare the city. God seems to have liked the idea because she dropped dead – a white lily blossoming from her blood as she did so.

**27th May** St Augustine of Canterbury was the first Archbishop of Canterbury and the first English prelate, at least in the south where Roman Christianity seems to have died out. Whilst on his way to Britain to evangelise the pagans he got frightened by the stories of the nasty English (all true of course) and scampered back to Rome. Here he asked the Pope (Gregory the Great no less) if he could go somewhere nicer, but the Pope was very cross and told him he HAD to go to England. So he did.

**30th May** It's St Joan of Arc's day today. I'm sure I needn't bore you with the details of her life and her fight to overthrow English rule in France and restore the French royal line, but I did want to mention one thing. During the First World War the US Treasury department issued a series of patriotic posters urging the women of America to buy War Saving Stamps to help the war effort. The most famous of these showed Joan of Arc under the stirring headline 'Joan of Arc Saved France'. They were apparently blissfully unaware that Joan had saved France from their allies – the British.

**31st May** St Petronilla has her day today. Medieval hagiographies claimed that she was the daughter of St. Peter and was so beautiful that he locked her up in a tower to keep the men away, but the Catholic Church has dismissed this (well they would wouldn't they). Tradition also has it that a pagan king called Flaccus wooed her. He presumably had a key to her tower (as it were). But she wasn't impressed with the nasty pagan and refused all his advances. When he absolutely insisted on marrying her, she went on hunger strike and died three days later. She should have stuck to the Eucharist Diet! (see 26th May). She is the patron saint of treaties between Frankish emperors and Popes – which is, let's be honest, quite a niche patronage – and, given the lack of Frankish emperors these days, leaves her with plenty of time on her hands.

# EUROPEAN LANGUAGES

## No. 3: Spanish

Spanish is the third most widely spoken language in the world after Mandarin Chinese and English. The Spanish alphabet has 30 letters as compared to 26 in English and about 50,000 characters in Chinese.

In Spanish the word *esposas* means both 'wives' and 'handcuffs'. The word *matador* is Spanish for 'killer'. The Spanish for a restaurant bill is *dolorosa*, meaning 'painful', and 'hummingbird' is *chupamirtos* (literally 'a suck-myrtles').

The Spanish are a proud people, and their language reflects this, endowing the humble with magnificent nomenclature. An *escaparatista* is not an escapologist but a window-dresser. An escapologist is an *evasionista*, rather than a tax-dodger. The romantic-sounding *fontanero* means plumber (literally 'spring-man'). It's also used in political slang to mean someone who investigates leaks. A plumber's mate goes by the sonorous title of *desatascador de fregaderos*, which sounds like a Spanish Admiral of the Fleet but in fact just means 'unblocker of sinks'. A *balconero* is not someone who hires a box at the opera but a cat burglar and a *zapador* is someone who uses a spade for a living (like 'sapper' in English).

\* \* \*

## SPANISH DICTIONARY

| | |
|---|---|
| baldada | bucketful |
| bolso | bag |
| bombo | gobsmacked |
| juicioso | wise |
| kodak | a small camera |
| pluto | sloshed |
| podredumbre | pus |
| propaganda | advertising |
| zambo | knock-kneed |
| zambombo | yokel |
| zambombazo | bang, explosion |

## SPANISH PHRASEBOOK

**Así te tragues un pavo y todas las plumas se conviertan en cuchillas de afeitar**
May all your turkey's feathers turn into razor blades

**Estoy hasta los cojones de este jodido hijo de puta**
I'm fed up to the male organs of generation with this very badly damaged son of a lady of ill repute

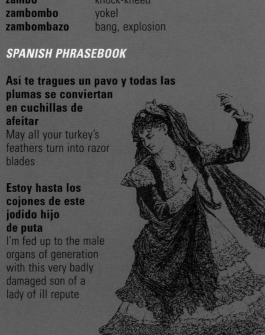

# ELVIS FROM A WELSH VIEWPOINT
## BY ROB BRYDON

There exist recordings of Elvis singing the following Beatles songs – 'Yesterday', 'Something', 'Get Back', 'Lady Madonna' and a particularly ill-advised stab at 'Hey Jude' in a key not fit for human consumption.

Songs about Elvis: 'Black Velvet' (Alannah Myles), 'King of the Mountain' (Kate Bush), 'Advertising Space' (Robbie Williams), 'Jordan the Comeback' (Prefab Sprout), 'Walking in Memphis' (Marc Cohn), 'Calling Elvis' (Dire Straits). Paul Simon says his song 'Graceland' is not about Elvis. Hmm... he's obviously not listened to it.

While playing in Memphis on his Born to Run tour in 1976, Bruce Springsteen scaled the wall at Graceland, hoping to visit Elvis and present him with the song 'Fire', written with the King in mind. Elvis wasn't in – he was performing in Lake Tahoe, and Bruce was escorted off the premises by a security guard. In the end the song was released by The Pointer Sisters.

Elvis was a big fan of Monty Python and Peter Sellers.

The American Secret Service's code name for President Clinton was 'Elvis'.

When Clinton played his saxophone on a US chat show, the tune was 'Heartbreak Hotel'.

Of George Bush, Clinton said: 'You know, Bush is always comparing me to Elvis in sort of unflattering ways. I don't think Bush would have liked Elvis very much, and that's just another thing that's wrong with him.'

The last song, 'It's Easy for You', on Elvis's last album, *Moody Blue*, was written by Tim Rice and Andrew Lloyd Webber.

In Las Vegas in the 1950s Elvis saw Billy Ward and the Dominoes performing a version of his then hit 'Don't Be Cruel'. He was so taken with it that he began to sing it just like the version he'd heard. If you listen to his live performances of the song he often sings the line 'at least please telephone' in the style he'd heard: 'at least please uh telephone'. It's very difficult to explain in print, but you can hear it on *The Million Dollar Quartet*. The singer in the Dominoes who performed the song was a then unknown Jackie Wilson. Elvis talked about Wilson's unique dance style. Years later, in one of his many films, when Elvis sang 'Return to Sender', he danced in the Jackie Wilson style. Incidentally, when Dexy's Midnight Runners played the Van Morrison song 'Jackie Wilson Said' on *Top of the Pops*, the BBC mistakenly put up a picture of Jocky Wilson, the popular darts player.

After visiting Graceland in 2004, I left my camera in a photo booth in a Memphis amusement arcade. When I went back it was gone. Do you have it?

**ELVIS WAS OF WELSH DESCENT. BOTH HIS PARENTS HAD WELSH CHRISTIAN NAMES. HIS MOTHER WAS CALLED GLADYS LOVE SMITH, AND HIS FATHER WAS CALLED VERNON ELVIS PRESLEY.**

The tiny parish of St Elvis is less than 20 miles from the Preseli Hills in Pembrokeshire, South Wales.

*The igneous rhyolite and dolerite 'bluestone' of the Preseli Hills is said to have provided the altar and ring stones for Stonehenge, which were were supposedly transported there by land and water. But similar stones have been discovered across southern Wales and England and even on Salisbury Plain itself.*

About 4 miles from St Davids, St Elvis is on the shore of St Bride's bay in St George's Channel. The small rather undistinguished church is dedicated to St Teilaw.

*St David, the patron saint of Wales, had an older cousin named 'Ailfyw' (the Welsh rendering of Elvis), who was once Bishop of Munster in Ireland and was famous for baptising St David at Porthclais.*

In Welsh, the village of St Elvis is known as Llaneilfyw (Church of Elvis). In 1833 it had a population of 44 people spread over two farms and 200 acres.

*Near Solva, 3 or 4 miles east of St Davids, there is a 'St Elvis Farm' which lies close to the 5,000-year-old St Elvis cromlech. The site of the former St Elvis Church and St Elvis Holy Well are also nearby. Local islands off the coast near Solva bear the name St Elvis Rocks.*

'Elvis foot' is climber's jargon for being so tired that your foot trembles on the rock.

*One of St Elvis's few recorded utterances seems to indicate a tolerance of homosexuality.*

In 1955, Elvis Presley was signed to the record company RCA. Though he had not yet had a hit record, he was paid $40,000, at that time the highest transfer fee ever paid to a recording artist.

*During his whole life, Elvis never went to the home of his manager 'Colonel' Tom Parker.*

*Right: Jackie Wilson, easily confused with (far right) Jocky Wilson*

# BIG SCIENCE FOR SMALL KITCHENS

# Experiments
## ...you can do at home

The elite QI research cadre doesn't spend all day with its noses in books. We are on a constant mission to understand and to measure the real world around us. Here, five senior 'action elves' demonstrate three experiments you can try at home. And one that you won't want to bother with as it is a completely futile waste of time, money and cats.

## 1: How to Measure the Speed of Light

**You will need:**
A microwave oven
A ruler
Some grated cheese*

**Step 1:** Disable the turntable on your microwave by removing the turntable or flipping the dish over. The experiment will not work if the cheese is rotating.

**Step 2:** Spread the grated cheese evenly on a plate and put the plate in the microwave.

**Step 3:** Turn microwave on for around 20 seconds. As soon as you see some of the cheese start to melt, STOP.

**Step 4:** Examine the grated cheese. You will see that some areas have melted and others haven't. Now measure the horizontal distance between the melted spots.

**Step 5:** Retire to perform your calculations.

**The calculations**
*Microwaves are electromagnetic waves tuned to 2.5 GHz – the exact frequency to make water molecules rotate. The rotation causes friction and the friction heats the food. Now, the one thing everyone knows about microwave ovens is that they don't heat things evenly. This is usually a bad thing, but for us it's really useful.*

*The key element in our measurement is that the microwaves in the oven are 'standing waves' – that is, they are stationary in space with only the amplitude (the up and down bit) oscillating. Microwaves heat at the high and low points of the wave only (that's why they heat so unevenly and why the food inside is usually rotated).*

*A wavelength is the distance from one wavetop to the next. So we can measure the length of the wave, which will be twice the distance between the melty spots in the cheese (as they melted at both the top and the bottom of each wave). Now that we have the wavelength of the microwaves (and we already know their frequency) we can calculate the speed of light using the following equation:*

*Speed of light = frequency x wavelength*

**So:**
*Wavelength (in metres) x frequency (in Hz) = speed of light (in metres per second)*

**Or, more cheesily:**
*Twice the distance between melty spots (in metres) x 2,500,000,000 (frequency in Hz) = SPEED OF LIGHT*

**Final Step:** *Eat cheese*
*\*chocolate chips are an acceptable substitute*

## 2: How to Measure the Circumference of the Earth

Eratosthenes first devised this experiment in the 3rd century BC. Are you as good with your hands as an ancient Greek? Let's find out.

**You will need:**
A piece of string
A protractor
A clock
A stick
A friend with a piece of string, a protractor, a clock and a stick
A sunny day

**Step 1:** Your friend needs to be on roughly the same longitude as you (i.e. due north or due south) but a few hundred miles away – and also in the northern hemisphere. Ghana is nice and sunny.

**Step 2:** Agree between you on a day to perform the experiment. Remember it must be sunny – so perhaps plump for summer?

**Step 3:** On that day, at exactly midday GMT, both go outside and place a stick vertically on the ground (your protractor may help with the verticality, or you could use a plumb bob or a spirit level). Take the string and hold it taut between the top of the stick and the end of the shadow it casts on the ground, forming a triangle.

**Step 4:** Measure the angle between the top of the stick and the string using your protractor. This is the angle at which the sun's rays are reaching the Earth.

**Step 5:** Retire indoors to phone your friend to get their measurement. Or you could use your mobile right where you're standing. Very much your choice.

**The calculations**
*For this calculation, we are going to assume that the sun is SO far away that the light rays hitting the Earth are effectively parallel. At midday at two different longitudes we measured the sun's angle in the sky using sticks and strings. These measurements will be different because the world is spherical(-ish).*

*The difference in angle will tell us what proportion of the 360 degrees of a full circle the slice between our two observers is. By finding out that proportion and multiplying it by the distance between the observers we can then calculate the circumference of the Earth.*

**Let's do the sums…**

**Step 1:** *The first thing we need to calculate is the difference between the two readings. Take the higher number (lets call it Angle 'a') and subtract the other reading (lets call that one 'b') from it. This tells us how many degrees of a circle there are between the two observers.*

**Step 2:** *Now we need to find out how many of those arcs would make up a full circle so let's divide it into 360. This tells us how many of the arcs between our observers it would take to make a full circle.*

**Step 3:** *Now we need to know the distance (we'll call it 'd') between the observers. You should be able to look this up online or in an atlas.*

**Step 4:** *Multiply this distance by the number you got in Step 2 and you've got the circumference ('C') of the Earth! Roughly. Hurrah! Treat yourself to more cheese.*

**To put it in mathematical terms:**

$$C = d \times [360/(a - b)]$$

Should you now wish to show off, you might care to calculate the surface area and volume of the Earth. You'll need first to calculate its radius 'r' using your measurement of the circumference C. This equation will do the trick:

$$r = C/2\pi$$

The surface area of the Earth will then be $4\pi r^2$ and the volume will be $v = 4/3\ (\pi r^3)$

### 3: How to Extract Your Own DNA

**You will need:**
- Yourself
- 1 tablespoon of salt
- 3 or 4 tablespoons of water
- Diluted washing-up liquid
- Some (very cold) gin (or vodka)
- A receptacle like a glass beaker
- A stirrer

**Step 1:** Mix the salt and water together to make salty water.

**Step 2:** Swish the salty water around your mouth, being careful not to swallow too much. Spit it back into the glass. It will now be swimming with DNA from your cheeks.

**Step 3:** Dip the stirrer first in the washing up liquid and then in the glass. Stir gently.

**Step 4:** Very carefully dribble a small amount of neat alcohol (the gin or vodka) down the inside of the glass. You might want your local cocktail waiter to help you with this. Hold the glass at a slight angle: you want the alcohol to sit atop the salty water. Keep going until you have a 2cm layer of alcohol.

**Step 5:** Stand by and wait. The DNA in the solution will find its way into the alcohol in the form of small white strands. This is the very essence of you, the unique code that makes you what you are.

**Why it works:**
*By swishing the salty water you have displaced some cells from the inside of your cheeks. These cells contain your DNA, which is released by the washing-up liquid because the soap breaks down the fatty membranes that make up the cell walls. The DNA strands are then free to migrate gradually up to the alcohol and clump together while other cell parts dissolve in the alcohol.*

**Final step:**
*Either use the DNA to create a thousand clones of yourself and take over the world, or send it to the police in case they ever want to convict you of something, or drink the gin (or vodka) with ice, tonic and a twist of lime. Or all three.*

## And here's that experiment we DON'T think you should try at home.

Operation 'Acoustic Kitty' was a CIA experiment in the 1960s in which they bugged a cat in the hope that it would eavesdrop from window sills, park benches and the like. It cost about £10 million to wire up the first cat, and five years of experimenting before it was ready. It was then run over by a taxi.

# AUNTY JO'S PROBLEM PAGE

*Dear Aunty Jo,*
*I am a married woman in my forties with three children. Both my husband and I work full-time. Consequently, my house is very untidy and dirty. Do you have any tips?*
*Love, Betty.*

Dear Betty,

If you can hang on for a while, I am in the process of writing a book for the stressed housewife called *Fuck It, That'll Do.* This will help you cut corners to the point of not doing any housework at all. But do bear in mind you can always clean the house when you retire. Let's be honest, nobody is going to look back over their life and say: 'Oh dear, the house was very messy on the third Tuesday after Whitsun 1991,' are they? I also find alcohol helps to dull the nagging voice of Mrs Domestic Goddess in your head.

Good luck!
Love, Aunty Jo

*Dear Aunty Jo,*
*Why are men so crap at multitasking?*
*Love from Ted.*

Dear Ted,

I think you'll find this is because they do things so thoroughly. Last week, I popped to the shops and asked my husband to tidy the front room while I was out. When I came back, all the furniture was in the garden and he was using an attachment on the Hoover I've never even bloody seen before. Excuse my inappropriate language, but it was very irritating.

Yours, Aunty Jo

*Dear Aunty Jo,*
*Is there a God?*
*Love, Bernard Manning.*

Dear Bernard,
Yes, there is. She is a fat black woman in a wheelchair.

Love, Aunty Jo

*Dear Aunty Jo,*
*I have an irritating itch on my left side.*
*Love from Stephen.*

Dear Stephen,
That is Alan.
Love, Aunty Jo

*Dear Aunty Jo,*

*I am on a television show called QI and I keep coming last. What shall I do?*
*Love, Alan.*

Dear Alan,
As you are quite attractive, I think a sex change might help. Then all you need to do is smile becomingly and giggle a bit and people will ignore the fact your minus score has gone into free fall. Your other alternative is to overturn thousands of years of misogynist expectation single-handedly, which might take a bit longer.
Good luck!
Aunty Jo

*Dear Aunty Jo,*
*I have a very small penis. What can I do?*
*love from*
*(Name and*
*address supplied)*

Dear Jeremy Clarkson of Chipping Norton,
It's what we all expected.
Love, Aunty Jo

*Aunty Jo*

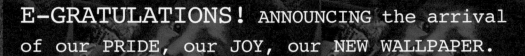

# E-GRATULATIONS! ANNOUNCING the arrival of our PRIDE, our JOY, our NEW WALLPAPER.

*EMILY ROSARIO PERLMUTTER BORN: ?? 2007 in GUATEMALA*
*ARRIVED HOME: January 25th, 2008 to the loving carbon-neutral arms of WENDY and ROSS PERLMUTTER*

Isn't she precious? Please note that the picture is a result of conversion for viewing on your screen and in no way represents Emily's true pigmentation. If you wish to print off Emily's pic, please, please use recyclable paper.

ABOUT HER NATURAL PARENTS: All I can say is Emily now has a real family, not a pretend one. Nothing against the Guatemalans (those pan-flute bands are amazing) but whereas her real mother gave her a nationality, we are here to give her the World… and to teach her how to protect it!

A FUTURE FOR OUR CHILD: Every child, no matter how precious, leaves a teensy tiny carbon footprint. During adoption proceedings, Ross and I made seven round-trip flights to Guatemala City. Calculated at 5 tons $CO_2$ emissions per person per trip* that comes out to – well, you do the math – 70 tons! To give you an idea of how much $CO_2$ that is, imagine drinking 64,000 Pepsis (Diet or Regular) a day for the rest of your life. Thus you can see that Emily arrives in this world with quite a substantial $CO_2$ debt on her little shoulders. Let's start planting those trees people!

A VISIT: Emily can't wait to see all her new friends and admirers! We strongly insist if you plan to pay a visit, please 'green' it. Carpooling is highly recommended. Ross is organizing a VanPool (hybrid 8-seater) for next Tuesday, February 1st at 4:00 p.m. Just let us know if you want a ride.

GIFTS: Riddle – what kind of showers don't carry acid rain? Answer: Baby showers! (LOL). They can, however, impact on nature in other insidious ways, so be very careful what you choose to bring as a gift. No gratuitous wrapping paper, ribbons or bows please. I don't need to tell you what that's doing to our forests. We recommend 100% cotton clothing, dye-free and of course any baby wear made from recyclable products. No Nike or Baby Gap stuff. The jury's still out on their 'fair-trade' claims. We really want to keep little Emily logo-free. And oh yes, Gina Ford books are strictly no-go in our household. That woman's murdered a lot of trees with her Nazi child-rearing manifestos.

In fact we would like to suggest a wonderful alternative: Ross has set up a carbon-offset account in Emily's name. Why not forgo those Teletubbies and fluffy booties and make a donation in Emily's name to the Vivo Project of Uganda which is currently attempting to build a wood-fired biomass boiler which operates on a 30 kilowatt photovoltaic turbine system!! Little Emily will love you for it!

THE BIG QUESTION – CLOTH VS. DISPOSABLE: Ross and I have agonized endlessly over what kind of impact Emily's diaper usage (a period we conservatively estimated to be 2 years) will have on the environment. Obviously we will eschew disposable diapers, given that a billion trees per year are cut down to make the wood pulp for disposables, not to mention the bleach used to whiten them producing organochlorine (Dioxin: the primary ingredient of Agent Orange! And you thought baby poop was toxic!).

Unfortunately, cloth diapers, though recyclable, utilize a large number of pesticides and chemicals to harvest the cotton they're made from. Even more detrimentally, washing them would use approximately 30,000 gallons of water annually – a cumulative total of 75,000 gallons of water. My, what a dilemma! After some serious back and forth on the issue, we realized maybe introspection was the answer: Physician heal thyself, if you will. By calculating that Ross and I personally flush about 60,000 gallons per year down the toilet the solution became obvious: all three of us are going to wear cloth diapers for the next two years. By our calculations, this will result in a net gain of 90,000 gallons of water per year.

A FEW FINAL WORDS: Having endured fourteen failed in-vitros, Ross and I were having a tough time understanding what was happening to us. We felt Nature had singled us out for punishment. We now appreciate that Ross's nugatory sperm yield was not a cruel twist of Nature, but in fact a Hidden Blessing (though I still maintain it's the result of a lifetime of ingested pollutants and industrial effluvia on Ross's part). The Adoption Process, for us, was clearly meant to be. Parenthood is a path, no matter how one arrives at it, though we both could have done with a little less paperwork and a more expeditious delivery. I know you're all sick of seeing us in those matching 'Expecting from Guatemala' T-shirts. Take our word for it – the wait was worth it!

**\* \* \* \***

*\* The 5 tons of $CO_2$ per person is a conservative estimate based on a full plane. In fact, the flights we took to Guatemala City were only half-full, so a truer calculation would be 7.5 tons of $CO_2$ emissions per person. However, Ross and I are not going to accept undue blame. It's not our fault if Guatemala City is a shithole and no one wants to fly there!*

Love from Wendy and Ross

## EMILY

## FROM RICH HALL'S JUNKMAIL FOLDER

Where's Johnny?

67

# Egghead Corner

*Firstly, which eighteenth century do we mean? It's not enough to say '1701 to 1800'. Historians speak of a 'short' and a 'long' eighteenth century. The first fits somewhere inside the calendar dates of the real century, the second overhangs both ends of the calendrical one.*

*The 'short' and 'long' centuries are defined by the events that bookmark the key developments of the period, and these depend on the tastes and cultural prejudices of whichever historian is doing the defining. For example, the 'long' eighteenth century can mean the entire period between 1688 (Britain's Glorious Revolution) and 1832 (the passing of the Reform Act).*

*For QI purposes, we will consider a 'smudged' eighteenth century, which contains all the events of the 100 years but leaks a bit around the borders.*

**LISTS:** The great linguistic achievement of the eighteenth century was Dr Samuel Johnson's *Dictionary of the English Language*, published in April 1755 after nine years of compilation. It was not the first dictionary of the English language, though. That was arguably Richard Mulcaster's 8,000-word *Elementarie* (1582). In a separate development, Mulcaster, a headmaster by profession, also gave the world the word 'football' and was the first person to describe its metamorphosis into a team sport (compared to the near-riot that it had been in early Tudor times).

Mulcaster's aim was to stabilise the 'hard words' in the English language, which he believed could supplant Latin in education. In his foreword he wrote: 'I do not think that anie language, be it whatsoever, is better able to utter all arguments, either with more pith, or greater planesse, than our English tung is, if the English utterer be as skillfull in the matter, which he is to utter.'

All of which shows the chaotic flux of everyday spelling before Johnson's *Dictionary* came on the scene. By Johnson's time, Mulcaster's optimism had been rewarded: mass literacy was on the rise, and the world needed an English-language 'rulebook'. Johnson's great achievement was to take a 'family portrait' of the language at the time, illustrated with quotations that would clarify every usage he described. Naturally, the book was huge in every sense. The first edition had 2,300 pages that were 46 inches tall and 56 inches wide, and came in two volumes (A–K and L–Z), together weighing 20 pounds.

However, Johnson's achievement is dwarfed by the publication (completed in 1725) of dynastic China's answer to the *Encyclopaedia Britannica*. This was the Gujin Tushu Jicheng, which translates into the modest claim: 'Complete Collection of Illustrations and Writings from the Earliest to Current Times'. Weighing in at 800,000 pages, spread over 10,000 individual scrolls, it was the first major publication in China to be set in movable copper type and contained 100 million individual Chinese characters. Only 60 copies were ever produced.

**TOURETTE'S SYNDROME:** Johann Sebastian Bach died aged 65 in 1750, seven years before Dominico Scarlatti (aged 72) and nine years before Georg Frideric Handel (aged 74), all three composers having been born in 1685. Of the three, only Scarlatti had not gone blind after being operated on by an English quack named John Taylor. Scarlatti's compositions are catalogued with K-numbers, his K30 being the so-called 'Cat Fugue', which was supposedly based on a theme produced when his cat walked across the keyboard of his harpsichord. The 'K' in question is American musicologist Ralph Kirkpatrick, who compiled the definitive list of Scarlatti's works during the 1930s and 1940s.

The other composer whose works are catalogued with K-numbers is Joannes Chrysostomus Wolfgangus Theophilus Mozart, who was born in 1756 and who died of an unknown complaint in 1791, leaving over 600 compositions to posterity. The 'K' associated with Mozart's

work is Ludwig (Ritter) von Köchel, who published his catalogue of the composer's work in 1862. Mozart's first two baptismal names (Joannes Chrysostomus) are from the patron saint of 27th January (his birthday), John Chrysostom. 'Chrysostom' was added to the name of St John of Antioch (c.350–400) to distinguish him from several other St Johns, and the word itself means 'Goldenmouth', in reference to the eloquence and piety of his preaching.

In other words, St John had little in common with Mozart, whose potty-mouthed outbursts are legendary. St John Chrysostom once wrote: 'What good is it if the Eucharist table is overloaded with golden chalices when your brother is dying of hunger? Start by satisfying his hunger and then with what is left you may adorn the altar as well.' Mozart once wrote a song called 'Lick out My Arse'. Mozart was very odd. He was physically pained by the sound of a trumpet and clung to childhood rituals such as strict bedtimes. Eyewitness accounts describe him fidgeting endlessly, talking nonsense and miaowing like a cat while jumping on furniture, apparently not caring that his behaviour was strange to everyone else. Behaviour such as this has earned him (along with Dr Johnson) a speculative 'diagnosis' of Tourette's Syndrome. If such analysis is correct, Mozart had a very rare form of the syndrome. Fewer than 1% of Touretters are compulsively obscene in their 'tics'. We will never know, not least because Tourette's Syndrome was only first described in 1895.

The middle name 'Amadeus' is merely a Latinised version of Mozart's Greek-derived forename Theophilus, meaning 'loved by God'. It comes from a period in the 1770s in which he toured Italy, calling himself variously 'Wolfgang Amadè' or 'Wolgang Amadeo' in order to ingratiate himself with the locals. He never referred to himself as 'Amadeus', although he did sign his marriage certificate with 'Amadè' when he got married to Constanze Weber and once, in a light-hearted personal letter, as 'Wolfgangus Amadeus Mozartus' (also adding the cod-Latin '-us' suffix to each word of the date on which he was writing).

**DIVING:** Given the name 'Sir Edmond Halley' (pronounced 'Haw-ley'), most people will not recognise it. When you mispronounce it as 'HAL-ee', more people will recognise it and most of them will immediately mention comets. They might spell his first name 'Edmund' too, but that's their problem. While it is true that, in 1707, Sir Edmond Halley predicted the return of a comet that now bears his surname, he did other things as well: such as inventing (in 1690) and testing (in 1717) the world's first diving bell. The trial took place in the Thames. Sir Edmond and five fellow researchers remained submerged at a depth of 60 feet for nearly two hours. During this time, their atmosphere was replenished by sealed barrels of London air sent down on weighted cables.

Sir Edmond was also (and rather embarrassingly for science-worshippers) a founder and diehard proponent of the 'Hollow Earth' theory. The Auroras Borealis and Australis were, in his view, likely to be the escape of ionised gases from holes at the Earth's poles. Inside the Earth were four other spheres, nested like Russian *Matrioshka* dolls, roughly corresponding to the sizes of Venus, Mars and Mercury.

**HEIGHT:** In the eleventh century, the average height of a European male was just over 5 feet 8 inches (1.73 metres). Over the next two centuries, this fell slightly to just under 5 feet 7 inches (1.7 metres) but, by the eighteenth century, it had dropped to under 5 feet $5\frac{1}{2}$ inches (1.662 metres). The cause was probably poor crops and diseases resulting from the Little Ice Age (LIA).

The eighteenth century marked the high point (or rather low point) of the LIA, a dip in the Earth's temperature that began at some point between 1200 and 1500 and ended between 1850 and 1900. The resultant crop failures (and the consequent skyrocketing of the price of flour) are the likely culprit for the bread riots that supposedly led Marie Antoinette to say 'Then let them eat cake'. But, if she ever said it at all – which is very unlikely – she certainly wasn't the first.

For a start, the legendary quote is *Qu'ils mangent de la brioche* ('Then let them eat brioche') and for a finish, Book Six of Jean-Jacques Rousseau's 12-volume autobiographical work *Confessions* was written around 1767 and contains the following passage: 'At length I recollected the thoughtless saying of a great princess, who, on being informed that the country people had no bread, replied, "Then let them eat pastry!"' Whoever this 'great princess' was, it wasn't Marie Antoinette, who first arrived in France from her native Austria in 1760 – the same year Rousseau's *Confessions* were published.

---

* For people who think pictures in books are a little bit babyish.

**A HIPPO DOES NOT HAVE A STING IN ITS TAIL, BUT THE WISE MAN PREFERS TO BE SAT ON BY A BEE** (POLISH)

**REVOLUTIONS:** There were three major revolutions in the eighteenth century: the French Revolution, the American Revolution and the Industrial Revolution. All historians agree that the American Revolution happened in 1776 and the French one in 1789, but when the Industrial one happened appears to be a matter of opinion. It either began in 1780 (Eric Hobsbawm), or in 1760 (T. S. Ashton), or it had already started by around 1400 with the invention of the printing press and was just a bit slow to get going (Lewis Mumford).

France, at that time still ruled by a monarchy, was the key ally of the fledgling American nation, mainly because it annoyed the British so much. The French supplied arms and ships to the revolutionaries until the final victory in 1783. France gained very little from the whole affair. In fact, seeing as the French monarchy was overthrown by a mob inspired by the American Revolution you could actually say that the French did as badly out of it as the British.

The Glorious Revolution, as discussed, can be said to mark the start of the long eighteenth century, but since it wasn't very glorious and it wasn't really a revolution (more of a coup d'état with the aim of installing a Dutch Protestant on the English throne), we'll let that pass.

**PIRACY:** The eighteenth century saw the Golden Age of Piracy, which started in 1716 and lasted until 1826 or 1830 or 1850, depending on whom you listen to. This was partly due to the high unemployment rate among European sailors following the signing of the Treaty of Utrecht, which ended the Spanish War of Succession and meant naval budgets could safely be cut back. It was also partly due to the expansion of the colonial supply lines in the Atlantic and Pacific, with cargo ships sailing back and forth to ferry the riches of the frontiers back to their European homes – a development which may in turn have been driven by the widespread crop failures in Northern Europe noted above. As twentieth-century economists have apparently so far failed to notice, high unemployment + expanding prosperity = rising crime.

Another lesson that hasn't been learned is that speculation without sound foundations – as happened during the South Sea Bubble – leads to a crash. The South Sea Bubble was inflated by the excitement at the opening up of the new trade routes. Suddenly, it seemed, there would be fantastic opportunities to get filthy rich if one invested one's money in the South Sea Company, which was backed with £10,000,000 by the Government of George I – a sum beyond the dreams of eighteenth-century avarice and still enviable today. Unhappily, the same thought occurred to crooks, who promptly set up their own 'south sea' companies promising investors such delights as perpetual motion machines, the restoration of English vicarages and the establishment of a 'company for carrying on an undertaking of great advantage, but nobody to know what it is'. Shares in these ludicrous ventures sold like bread to pigeons, and before long the whole thing went 'pop', depriving many people of their savings and making a few rascals very rich indeed. The same thing happens in the present day, most obviously with the dotcom bubble of the 1990s. Far be it from the present, however, to suggest any similarities between market traders and pirates.

**COWS:** A cow called Blossom changed the course of world history in 1796, when she passed the disease of cowpox to a London dairymaid called Sarah Nelmes. A doctor called Edward Jenner took pus from her 'poxes' (blisters) and injected it into the arm of a nine-year-old boy called James Phipps. The result was that (after a short fever) Phipps became the first recorded human being to be deliberately inoculated against smallpox, a far deadlier disease that had ravaged the human race since time immemorial. Edward Jenner entered the history books by publishing his results in 1798 and giving the world the word 'vaccination' – derived from the Italian word 'vacca', meaning 'cow'. But was Phipps really the first inoculated human? Jenner had embarked on his experiments after hearing a well-attested piece of country lore to the effect that cowpox prevented smallpox, so there must have been other instances before. Indeed, a Dorset farmer called Benjamin Jesty had already done the same thing to his family by 1774. Rather sadly, Jenner was unsuccessful when he inoculated his own son, who later died of smallpox. Jenner was also the first scientist to state that hatchling cuckoos push the rightful eggs out of their host nests using a special hollow in their backs. Previously it had been believed that the adult cuckoo did this while the 'victim' bird wasn't looking. Jenner wasn't proven right until the advent of photography.

**KINGS:**
*George the First was always reckoned*
*Vile, but viler George the Second.*
*And what mortal ever heard*
*A good word of George the Third*
*But when from earth the Fourth descended*
*God be praised the Georges ended.*
(Walter Savage Landor, b. 1765)

George I, Elector of Hanover, inherited the English throne at the age of 54 thanks to the Act of Settlement (1701). This named his mother as the only eligible successor to the faltering English monarchy. There were actually fifty European royals with better claims, but none of them were Protestant. In 1720, the South Sea Company collapsed and the ensuing economic chaos made George and his ministers extremely unpopular. Robert Walpole was appointed First Lord of the Treasury in April 1721 to take care of the mess, and from this date forth the monarchy became less and less involved in government. George retreated into the arms of his mistresses, the fat Charlotte Sophia Kielmannsegge (whom he created Countess of Darlington) and the thin Eherngard Melusina von Schulenberg (created Duchess of Kendall). The two were more popularly known as 'The Elephant' and 'The Maypole'. George had imported them to Britain along with his wife, and they ransacked the jewellery boxes of Britain so thoroughly that George's wife had to be enthroned in hired glass. Their scrounging became so notorious that a torch-wielding mob waylaid their coach and threatened to sack it. 'Goot pippil!' called the Maypole in her thick German accent, 'Vot vor you abuze uz? Ve came for all your goots!' This prompted one wit to reply: 'Yes, and all our chattels too, damn ye!'

George I's son George II deserves a place in history as the only monarch whose heart has been overheard exploding. His valet reported hearing a louder report as the King sat on the lavatory on the morning of October 25th, 1760. This was followed by a heavy thump and a moan. The valet rushed in to find the stricken king sprawled dying on the floor. At autopsy, it was shown that a ventricle had burst in his heart and that this was the noise the valet had heard. Alas, his first son, Frederick, Prince of Wales, was not around to rejoice, having died of a burst abscess in his lung after being hit by a cricket ball ten years earlier. George and Frederick hated each other with a passion truly beyond measure, and after a row over allowances in 1736, George barred Frederick from the deathbed of his own mother, saying: 'Bid him go about his business, for his poor mother is not in a condition to see him act his false, whining, cringing tricks now, nor am I in a humour to bear his impertinence; and bid him trouble me with no more messages, but get out of my house.' Mind you, it was probably for the best. One of the last recorded utterances by Frederick's mother was about him: 'At least I shall have one comfort in having my eyes eternally closed – I shall never see that monster again.' (In life, she had once seen him through a window and shouted, 'Look! There he goes! That wretch! That villain! I wish the ground would open at this moment and sink the monster to the lowest hole in Hell!') The family's generally unsympathetic attitude towards the son known widely as 'Poor Fred' inspired a folk rhyme (recorded by William Makepeace Thackeray):
*Here lies Fred,*
*Who was alive and is dead.*
*Had it been his father,*
*I had much rather;*
*Had it been his sister,*
*No one would have missed her;*
*Had it been his brother,*
*Still better than another:*
*But since 'tis only Fred,*
*Who was alive and is dead,*
*Why, there's no more to be said.*

The throne next fell to Frederick's son, who became George III. Under his reign, Britain's most visionary poet, William Blake, flourished quietly and wrote the poem now known as 'Jerusalem', which was set to music in the early twentieth century by Hubert Parry. Blake was once ordered to cut the grass in his front garden by soldiers of King George III and replied: 'Damn the King and damn his soldiers, they are all slaves!' By contrast, when George V first heard Sir Edward Elgar's orchestration of Parry's setting of 'Jerusalem' in 1922, he said he wished it could become the national anthem instead of 'God Save the King'.

# WHAT GOES ON IN A BOFFIN'S BRAIN?

# The QI ENGINEER SIMULATOR

by Ted Dewan
(BSc Engineering)

**A**lthough you may appreciate the shiny things they design that go fast and make music, engineers (often simply referred to as 'They') subject you to ever more subtle forms of daily abuse as society becomes increasingly perverted by technology.

They work day and night to exploit every opportunity to humiliate the public, often concealing their aggression behind sensible-sounding unimpeachable practical explanations. 'Khegh-hegh-heghh!' They chuckle merrily as you stand in the rain for eternity, waiting at pelican crossings for permission to interrupt the flow of their motor vehicles. 'Hunh hunh hunnnh!' They snigger, savouring your delicious frustration as you attempt to set a digital alarm clock using only two buttons labelled with nonsense engineer words like 'mode' and 'enter'. '*Ha ha!*' They guffaw as you willingly part with another tenner on a guide that refers to you in its title as part of a widespread tribe of 'dummies' merely to comprehend one of their products. But what is it that causes such deviant behaviour in the sociopaths who create the systems that surround us?

You see, most sensible people wouldn't dream of serving their golden years of higher learning incarcerated in the fluorescent-lit gloom of a windowless engineering classroom. While the rest of the world youthfully frolics under the cherry blossom and snoozes in 'media studies', trainee engineers endure years of gruelling problem-solving and science-lab BO.

But once their brain-grinding apprenticeship is completed and the trainee engineers begin to flap their wet and sticky young wings, they gravitate towards the secretive international brotherhood of Them. Embedded within their dreary cubicles, They tirelessly shower the world with enslaving widgetry and extract their revenge on non-engineers for their frivolous merrymaking and ignorance. And so the non-technical public enters into a destructive cycle of dependency with the engineering fraternity, responding with untiring enthusiasm to the bogus promise of a better life through evermore developed technology while simultaneously increasing their psychological and physical dependency upon their products.

The engineer's vision of the world, however skewed, is consistent with the fruit of their disturbed and insular minds. Although it is clearly too late for most citizens of the technology-consuming societies to wean themselves off the goodies, it is never too late or hopeless to seek understanding and enlightenment, and perhaps attain some peace with the propellor-heads. Because in spite of the fact that They daily defecate upon the non-technical public through the medium of technology, They are largely to be pitied. Many engineers are victims of defects at birth, cursed with the likes of Geek Personality Disorder (GPD) and inadequate bodies that deviate substantially from optimum weight.

The QI Engineer Simulator gives you insight into the mental workings behind those who create the insults to dignity that are computer printers and retro toasters. It helps to understand the roots of the engineers' antisocial behaviour in order to forgive the boffins behind the bewildering devilry of burglar alarm control panels. They despise the non-technical public simply for the casual ease with which they succeed at being human. These poor creatures are only trying to make others feel stupid and inferior in an effort to persuade people that machines, and They who understand them, are in control of the world.

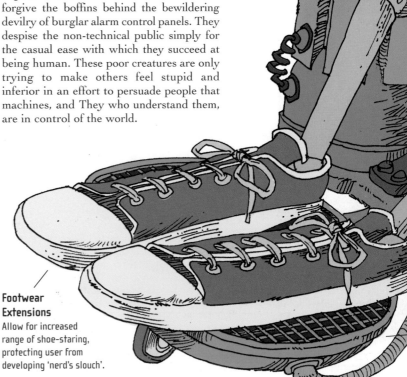

**Inamorata Aversion Relay**
External hormone detection unit directs user to masturbatory material so as not to waste time dealing with the social aspects of enchanting a sexual partner (coupled to *Libido Diverter*).

**Indifferent Sartorial Pattern Projector**
When projected upon plain, light-coloured material, creates the illusion of disastrous taste in clothing. User advised to wear plain white boiler suit for maximum fidelity of projected image. Choice pre-programmed by user's mum.

**RSS Tension Bands**
Simulates the symptoms of repetitive strain syndrome brought on by computer-based lifestyle, further enhancing obsession with one's own internal sensory environment.

**Moral Neutralysis Ballast Tank**
Facilitates cheerful obliviousness to the immoral consequences of user's actions while toiling with prolific abandon on over-engineered money-sucking delusional enterprises such as building weapons systems and transparent vacuum cleaners.

**Footwear Extensions**
Allow for increased range of shoe-staring, protecting user from developing 'nerd's slouch'.

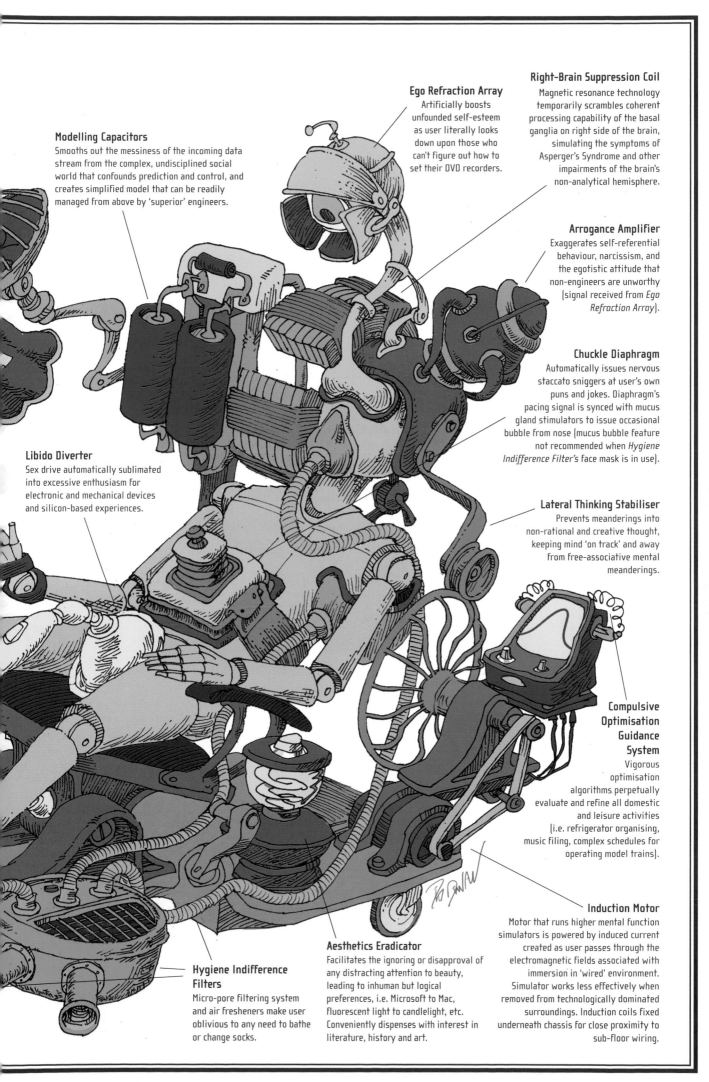

**Modelling Capacitors**
Smooths out the messiness of the incoming data stream from the complex, undisciplined social world that confounds prediction and control, and creates simplified model that can be readily managed from above by 'superior' engineers.

**Ego Refraction Array**
Artificially boosts unfounded self-esteem as user literally looks down upon those who can't figure out how to set their DVD recorders.

**Right-Brain Suppression Coil**
Magnetic resonance technology temporarily scrambles coherent processing capability of the basal ganglia on right side of the brain, simulating the symptoms of Asperger's Syndrome and other impairments of the brain's non-analytical hemisphere.

**Arrogance Amplifier**
Exaggerates self-referential behaviour, narcissism, and the egotistic attitude that non-engineers are unworthy (signal received from *Ego Refraction Array*).

**Chuckle Diaphragm**
Automatically issues nervous staccato sniggers at user's own puns and jokes. Diaphragm's pacing signal is synced with mucus gland stimulators to issue occasional bubble from nose (mucus bubble feature not recommended when *Hygiene Indifference Filter*'s face mask is in use).

**Libido Diverter**
Sex drive automatically sublimated into excessive enthusiasm for electronic and mechanical devices and silicon-based experiences.

**Lateral Thinking Stabiliser**
Prevents meanderings into non-rational and creative thought, keeping mind 'on track' and away from free-associative mental meanderings.

**Compulsive Optimisation Guidance System**
Vigorous optimisation algorithms perpetually evaluate and refine all domestic and leisure activities (i.e. refrigerator organising, music filing, complex schedules for operating model trains).

**Induction Motor**
Motor that runs higher mental function simulators is powered by induced current created as user passes through the electromagnetic fields associated with immersion in 'wired' environment. Simulator works less effectively when removed from technologically dominated surroundings. Induction coils fixed underneath chassis for close proximity to sub-floor wiring.

**Aesthetics Eradicator**
Facilitates the ignoring or disapproval of any distracting attention to beauty, leading to inhuman but logical preferences, i.e. Microsoft to Mac, fluorescent light to candlelight, etc. Conveniently dispenses with interest in literature, history and art.

**Hygiene Indifference Filters**
Micro-pore filtering system and air fresheners make user oblivious to any need to bathe or change socks.

# EBBREVIATIONS By Craig Brown

ET was a creature who tried to phone home,
ER is a monarch who sits on her throne.
EMU is the system controlled by Rod Hull,
ECT involves wires, attached to the skull.
EPO is a hormone — you will cycle like merde —
EH's what one says when one hasn't quite heard.
EX wants your money (and also your house),
EEK! oh my goodness! I just spied a mouse!
ERM is a mechanism or... um... hesitation,
ENO has no need for operatic translation.
ENO's also the producer of Bowie:
EG 'Boys Keep Swinging' — (now I'm just being showy).
EEC's both a trade group and lower-case poet,
ELO had a hit (but I'm damned if I know it).
ESA sends up rockets (but they're always unmanned),
ETA is the time we're unlikely to land.
ETA are terrorists, primarily Basque,
ETC indicates you're bored stiff with your task.
ENSA put on dresses to cheer up our lads,
EST it turned out was just one of those fads.
ESP means 'Hang on! I know what you're thinking',
E-mails I now manage to send without blinking.
E-numbers are terribly bad for the heart,
ETD is the time that the aircraft won't start.
EC is what EEC was (or was it EU?),
E17 were a boy band (but I preferred Blue).
EPs are recordings, neither albums or singles,
ELF registers the merest of tingles.
EMF is a novelist who makes most look inferior,
E-Coli potentially deadly bacteria.
ECG shows a line that bobs back and forth,
EE bah gum is the language they speak up in't North.
EMINEM's the white rapper who started a trend,
and that's all you're getting 'cos
this is the END.

EMU European Monetary Union ECT Electro-Convulsive Therapy EPO Erythropoietin ERM Exchange Rate Mechanism ENO English National Opera
EEC European Economic Community EEC Edward Estlin Cummings ELO Electric Light Orchestra ESA European Space Agency ETA Estimated Time of Arrival
ETA Euskadi Ta Askatasuna (Basque Country And Freedom) ENSA Entertainments National Service Association EST European Summer Time ESP Extra-sensory
Perception ETD Estimated Time of Departure ELF Extremely Low Frequency EMF Edward Morgan Forster ECG Electrocardiogram

# E-QUIZ

## WIN £1,000!

**WE'RE GIVING AWAY £1,000 IN CASH TO THE FIRST PERSON TO PROVIDE CORRECT ANSWERS TO THE EIGHTEEN QUESTIONS BELOW. EACH ANSWER IS A SINGLE WORD...**

For obvious reasons, the answers are not to be found in this book. To enter the competition – or simply to play the quiz for fun – visit www.qi.com/equiz

Follow the on-screen instructions. By typing your answers in the spaces provided, you'll be able to see your score immediately. You can play as many times as you like. When or if you score 100%, submit your answers online as instructed.

In the event of a draw, the winner will be the contestant who, in the opinion of the judges, provides the most interesting responses to questions 19–21. (For a chance of winning, it is advisable to attempt these tiebreakers.)

The winner and the eleven runners-up will be invited to a live recording of the QI 'F' Series to meet the stars of the show, followed by dinner with the QI Elves.

The deadline is 8.08 p.m. on the 8th of Eighpril '08. The winners will be notified by email within 8 days, and the answers will be posted on www.qi.com

To discuss the quiz and other quite interesting topics, visit www.qi.com/talk

## YOUR TIME STARTS NOW...

1. What is the word for the part of the play where the plot thickens?
2. Who or what are Dunk, Mya and Mary?
3. Which medicine comes from a Greek hedgehog?
4. What did zoologist Frank Buckland describe as 'horribly bitter'?
5. ADTFIAT, WUEMG. What does the 'E' stand for?
6. What connects two Kings of England, an estate in Kennington and a room in Kingsmeadow stadium?
7. Who is this? (See Below)
8. Which spherical object owes its name to the Ye river?
9. How many people could live off a day's oxygen from one acre of fir trees?
10. Where would you find a labyrinth, an oval window and a round window?
11. What is Mr A. G. Dorsey's preferred first name?
12. What is the next letter in the sequence:
    А, Б, В, Г, Д … ?
13. Who does this eye belong to? (See Below)
14. What was the 28th most popular name for baby girls in England and Wales in 2006?
15. Which country flies this flag? (See Below)
16. What did we eat 173 times in 2006?
17. Where would you see beaks going up Judy's passage?
18. What is a korvalappu?

### TIEBREAKERS
19. Tell us something Quite Interesting about Easington, County Durham.
20. Tell us something Quite Interesting about eagles.
21. Tell us something Quite Interesting about emails.

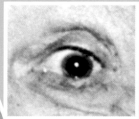

Whose eye is this? (Q13)

Who is this? (Q7)

Whose flag is this? (Q15)

73

The first known erotic texts appeared in China in 1200 BC. Perplexing instructions included 'Playing the Jade Flute' and 'Wailing Monkey Climbing a Tree'.

In ancient China, men developed a taste for tightly bound small feet. These were considered to be another sexual organ – they would bend them into a loop and have their way with them.

*~ not tonight..... I have a verruca.*

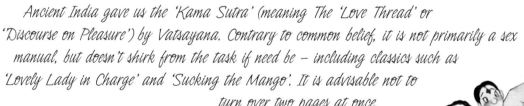

The Islamic world is rich in erotic literature, the most famous of which is 'The Perfumed Garden' by Sheikh Nefzawi. The explorer Sir Richard Burton (1821–1890) – who spoke 29 languages – translated it from the Arabic. Shortly after completing his revised version, he died. His wife Isabel burned it (and many of his other papers) before it could be published.

*~ well done, penis....*

In ancient Japan, erotic prints known as 'shunga' were commissioned by bordellos as advertisements. In 1002, Sei Shonagon, a lady at the Imperial Court, completed 'The Pillow Book' for the education of young women. Amongst many practical tips, wives are advised to praise their husband's penis.

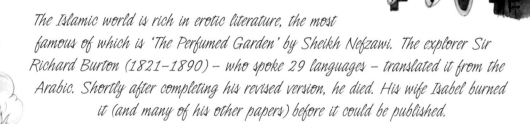

Ancient India gave us the 'Kama Sutra' (meaning The 'Love Thread' or 'Discourse on Pleasure') by Vatsayana. Contrary to common belief, it is not primarily a sex manual, but doesn't shirk from the task if need be – including classics such as 'Lovely Lady in Charge' and 'Sucking the Mango'. It is advisable not to turn over two pages at once.

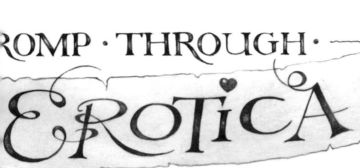

Ancient Greek erotica was rather more basic. Recommended positions included 'The Posterior Venus' and 'Hector's Horse'. Bottoms – male and female – loom large in Greek texts. According to legend, two sisters, blessed with beautiful big backsides, held a competition to decide which was the finer by flashing them at total strangers in the street. Hence the useful English word 'callipygian', meaning 'superbly bottomed'.

A little more recently, Giovanni Boccaccio (1313–1375) wrote the Decameron – 100 bawdy tales featuring disgraceful hanky-panky amongst the clergy.

The erotic poems of Robert Herrick (1591–1674) include 'Upon the Nipples on Julia's Breast' and 'Upon Julia's Sweat'.

The lewd verses of John Wilmot, Earl of Rochester (1647–1680), included 'Signior Dildo', a scandalous satire on the engagement of the future James II.

Giacomo Casanova (1725–1798) was actually rather a tragic figure with a weakness for women dressed in men's clothes.

Before settling down, late in life, to write his 'Life of Samuel Johnson', James Boswell (1740–1795) was a tremendous libertine, struggling with addictions to alcohol, gambling and prostitutes.

'This day show that you are Boswell, a true soldier. Take your post. Shake off sloth and spleen, and just proceed. Nobody knows your conflicts. Be fixed as a Christian, and shun vice. Go not to Amsterdam.'
JAMES BOSWELL, 'Journals', 1764

In modern China, 'blue' movies are yellow; in Japan they're green.
But surely they should be pink...

The difference between pornography and erotica is lighting.
GLORIA LEONARD

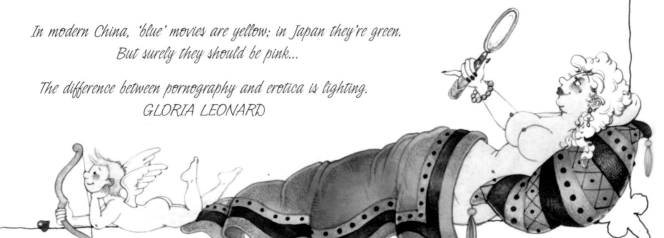

# ESSEX
## ALAN DAVIES

The road was typical of many in the area in that it was made up of good-sized detached houses for the aspirational middle classes. My Dad was a chartered accountant. When the railway reached Loughton in 1856, the Eastern Counties Railway did not allow 3rd-class ticket holders to board there or at any of the stations beyond it on the way to Epping. They didn't want the trains full of workers paying low fares, heaven forbid. That's why the North East London suburbs grew the way they did, with smaller houses closer to the centre in areas like Leyton and Walthamstow, from where workers were allowed to board the trains, and larger ones further out in places like Woodford and Loughton.

We pointed towards London because we were on the Central Line and we had an 01 telephone number, and because as teenagers we did not aspire to travel to Bishop's Stortford or Saffron Walden, nice as they are. We wanted to go to Camden Market and Carnaby St.

**This was partly because London was perceived as trendy and exciting, and partly because if you go too far north you can end up being anally raped in a Norfolk boys' school and that is much less fun than buying bootleg tapes of The Jam in Camden Town.**

Here is your introduction to my home county of Essex.
I will disavow you, is that right? Disinter? No. Er... challenge your preconceptions. Yes, that's it. Apologies in advance for having a preconception of your preconceptions, but I'm sticking to it. My bit of Essex points towards London. I grew up in Epping Forest. Actually, in a house near Epping Forest, in a road called Spring Grove in Loughton.

Norfolk?... Well I'll be buggered

WELCOME TO NORFOLK

I did venture out to Chelmsford and Southend to watch Essex play cricket. I was raised to enjoy cricket and I'd go with my older brother who would rather have gone alone. Chelmsford was capital of England for 5 days in 1381 when Richard II regained control of the country after the Peasants' Revolt. This is never mentioned at the cricket because I suspect no one knows about it. I have a cousin called Richard. He was called Dick until he rejected the name when he reached adolescence. Understandable. Cousin Richard is unrelated to Richard II, to my knowledge. Cricket excursions were always peaceful affairs. Leather on willow and all that. However, things have changed. During the modern floodlit Twenty20 games, boozy lads are liable to shout 'Jonathan' at me and then point their mobile phone cameras in my face. It's pointless telling them I'm not Jonathan Creek as they will only say 'Yes you are' and take more pictures.

**The atmosphere can become a little testy, and in those circumstances I shudder to recall the infamous match between Essex and Kent in 1776 when a spectator was bayoneted, a soldier was shot dead and one of the Kent players killed a member of the Essex team. The match took place at Tilbury Fort (built in 1672) and featured the worst violence the Fort ever saw.**

I don't think I like that phrase 'Richard II regained control of the country'. How was that done in 1381, when the peasants were revolting? I suspect it wasn't a matter of asking them nicely and was possibly more in the spirit of Tiananmen Square or Hungary in 1956. The peasants were revolting in Brentwood, which is now home to a posh private school. It also has good access to the M25. I was caught speeding on the M25 in 1987 and went to court in Brentwood. They said I was doing between 106 and 108 mph. In a subsequent stand-up routine I claimed that I then said, 'That'll be 107 then.' I didn't really. I was cowed into silence. The magistrates banned me for two weeks. At the next-door police station I asked how to get back to Loughton. They wouldn't tell me, so I got in my car and drove anyway,

thinking that if I was stopped I'd tell them I was going to a phone box to get help. Brilliant, I'm sure you'll agree. They watched me leave and arrested me after a 50-yard, *Life on Mars* pursuit with full flashing blue lights. While I was locked up in custody I was pitifully scared and realised I would be a rubbish criminal. A few weeks later I received a second ban (four weeks). Nowadays the police no longer have to watch through the window for miscreants flouting driving bans – in 1994 Brentwood became the first town in the UK to install colour CCTV.

**Essex has a history of zero tolerance for criminality. William Calcraft from Little Baddow exemplified this spirit. As Britain's longest-serving hangman, he is thought to have hanged between 400 and 450 people in a 45-year career. It sounds a lot until you realise it's less than one a month. Lazy Bill.**

Loughton is home to the Royal Mint, where all of Britain's bank notes are printed. When the M11 was being built, everyone I knew had 'Stop the M11' stickers in their cars. From Loughton it's only possible to gain access to the southbound carriageway. This is because there was a fear that if a gang robbed the Mint (in order to become minted) they could flee north up the M11 to an airfield. From there it's just a short hop to.... nowhere you can spend any pounds. As far as I know, the Mint has never been robbed but the potential is there. After all, more cars are broken into in Loughton than anywhere else in the UK. If Loughtonians are shocked and would like to move to a safer place, Southend is recommended as the safest large town in the UK, with just 30.91 crimes per 1,000 people.

> **While I was locked up in custody I was pitifully scared and realised I would be a rubbish criminal.**

Although Essex is generally safe, Britain's Best Earthquake shook the village of Wivenhoe in 1884. The chimney of the gasworks collapsed and masonry fell from the church tower. Records show that someone 'later died of shock'. That's not what shock means to me. Something that hits you later? No, no, no. You die of shock there and then: 'Aargh!' (thud). To die of shock 'later' suggests someone who had had a dream about an earthquake in which the chimney of the gasworks fell on him or his name was Mason and he fell off the church tower. Or something. Wivenhoe is tranquil enough now, but if you want real security you could book a spot in Kelvedon's nuclear bunker for £30,000. (This will secure you a place for 10 years.) Be warned, though. In the event of a nuclear attack, you may be joined by 600 government types.

Colchester lords it over Chelmsford as Britain's oldest town. It was probably for a time the capital of Roman Britain and has the distinction of being written about by Pliny the Elder in AD 77. He is generally as reliable as the interweb for information. He described it as Camulodunum, though I suspect he was dictating after too much bacchanalian revelry and was just trying to say Colchester. There has always been plenty of wine in Essex. Ten vineyards are currently operational, two more than in the 11th century. The star grape is the bacchus. The vineyards survived the late 20th century despite the countywide practice of only drinking wine at Christmas and traditionally drawing it from a cardboard box stored next to a radiator. It's the temperate climate that leads to all the wine-growing. St Osyth (never heard of it) is the driest place in the UK, with only 513 mm of precipitation per year. I've no idea how that compares to anywhere else, but I'm sure that if everyone in St Osyth went out and a had a pee in the garden they'd probably double it.

**Ignoring Colchester's rich history, Chelmsford leapt ahead in 1893 when The Eclipse, the world's first electric toaster, was invented there. Five years later Marconi opened the world's first 'wireless' factory.**

It seemed nothing could stop Chelmsford from taking its place at the hub of the world's burgeoning electronics industry. Sadly, progress halted on the opening of the world's first naturist site in a back garden in Wickford. A member of the English Gymnosophist Society made her garden available for naked air-bathing, and Essex, with its collective eye off the ball and on the balls, was soon electronically eclipsed by the Japanese.

Mistakes are still sometimes made – in 2003, a museum in Leigh-on-Sea was forced to abandon plans to exhibit a 150,000-year-old woolly mammoth tusk when a second opinion from a geologist identified it as a length of Victorian drainage pipe – but Essex has recovered from missing out on hundreds of billions of yen with a characteristic and innate cheeriness epitomised

by the dazzling smile of its three famous beauties: Vicki Michelle, out of *'Allo, 'Allo!*; Daniella Westbrook, out of *Eastenders*; and Jodie Marsh, out of her clothes. Where does that sense of humour come from? The answer is Braintree, home of Nicholas Udall who created England's first comedy, *Ralph Roister Doister*, in the early 1550s. He was also headmaster of Eton College but left in disgrace when he was accused of stealing a silver plate from the College Chapel.

*YOU CAN TAKE THE BOY OUT OF ESSEX BUT YOU CAN'T TAKE ESSEX OUT OF THE BOY...*

**THERE IS NO SUCH THING AS AN UGLY WOMAN, BUT THERE IS SUCH A THING AS NOT ENOUGH VODKA (RUSSIAN)**

**NOW SOME POETRY:**
*There was a young boy from Chelmsford*
*Who soon discovered the futility of trying to write a limerick about his home town as there is no word in English that rhymes with Chelmsford, apart from an obscure town in New York called Elmsford.*

**SO HE WROTE:**
*There was a young boy from Chelmsford*
*Who spent all his life in Chelmsford*
*He had a Capri*
*And a wife called Tracey*
*And they shared a house in Chelmsford.*

*Jodie Marsh, almost out of her clothes*

# EUROPEAN LANGUAGES

## No. 4: Italian

**That soft bastard Latin which melts like kisses from a female mouth.**　LORD BYRON

The Italian alphabet uses only 20 letters. There are hardly any words beginning with H, J, K, W, X or Y in an Italian dictionary and all of them are borrowed directly from other languages.

The Italian for 'pencil-sharpener' is *temperamatite*, a 'drug-addict' is *tossicodipendente* and 'goo' is *sostanza appiccicosa* ('sticky substance').

*Tasso* in Italian means both 'yew' and 'badger' and the Italian for a 'crack' is *botto*.

### ITALIAN DICTIONARY
The key divisions of the Italian language are as follows:

*1. Italian words that look convincingly Italian.*

| | |
|---|---|
| babbo | dad |
| baffo | moustache |
| bollo | stamp |
| bosso | box |
| buffo | funny |
| bullo | tough |
| buzzo | paunch |
| dotto | duct |
| fatto | fact |
| fitto | thick |
| flusso | flow |
| fosso | moat |
| frizzo | witticism |
| goffo | clumsy |
| golfo | gulf |
| gozzo | throat |
| grillo | cricket (grasshopper) |
| groppo | tangle |
| grullo | silly |
| gruppo | group |
| mozzo | buoy |
| tappo | cork |

| | |
|---|---|
| tatto | touch |
| tetto | roof |
| tocco | touch |
| tozzo | stocky |
| trucco | make-up |
| tutto | all |
| zoppo | wobbly |

*2. Italian words that look like English*

| | |
|---|---|
| bimbo | child |
| bonzo | Buddhist monk |
| brillo | pissed |
| bronco | bronchial tube |
| bruno | brown |
| frodo | contraband |
| garbo | grace |
| gobbo | hunchback |
| gonzo | dolt, simpleton |
| monaco | monk |
| montgomery | duffel-coat |
| tonto | stupid, dumb, silly |
| zappa | hoe |
| zeppo | jam-packed |

*3. Italian words that look like Finnish*

| | |
|---|---|
| battipanni | carpetbeater |
| bendisposto | well-disposed |
| bighellone | moocher |
| bussolotto | dice-shaker |
| frangiflutti | breakwater |
| fuggifugg | stampede |

*3. Italian words that look like German*

| | |
|---|---|
| krapfen | doughnut |
| transfert | transference |

*4. Italian words that are English but where some Italian's got the wrong end of the stick somewhere along the line.*

| | |
|---|---|
| big | an industrial mogul or movie star |
| boy | a male ballet dancer |
| flipper | a pinball machine |
| footing | jogging |
| miss | a beauty queen |
| mister | a professional body-builder |
| mole | a massive shape |

| | |
|---|---|
| tip tap | tap-dancing |
| torpedo | a touring car |

*5. Italian words that only Italians apparently feel the need for*

| | |
|---|---|
| balillo | a member of a Fascist youth group |
| bambolotto | a male doll |
| mammismo | an excessive attachment to one's mother |
| zampata | a blow from the paw of an animal |
| zimarra | a long shabby coat |
| zirlare | to sing like a thrush |
| zuzzurullone | an over-grown school kid |

*6. Wonderfully evocative Italian words*

| | |
|---|---|
| blatta | cockroach |
| buggerare | to swindle |
| friggere | to fry |
| tamponare | to plug |
| turlupinare | to cheat |
| zanzana | mosquito |
| zazzera | a shock of hair |
| zoccolo | hoof, clog |

*7. Peculiar Italian noises*

| | |
|---|---|
| bau bau | bow wow! |
| bum | boom! |
| tictac | tick-tock |

*8. God knows how these came about*

| | |
|---|---|
| boato | a roar |
| boato sonico | sonic boom |
| bradipo | sloth |
| zampognaro | bagpiper |

*9. Other stuff*

| | |
|---|---|
| bozzettista | sketch-writer |
| zenzero | ginger |
| zizzania | discord |
| zolphanello | match |
| zolletta | lump, cube |
| zoppicante | limping |

### ITALIAN PHRASEBOOK

**vai a farti friggere!**
get lost! (literally, 'go screw yourself')

# Lavatories
## THROUGH THE AGES

The world's oldest discovered lavatories date back to 2500 BC. The Harappan or Indus Valley civilisation, in what is now Pakistan, invented the first known basic flush system. They would tip a pot of water into a bowl with a hole that would wash the waste away through a pipe into an underground drain.

There were also quite advanced lavatories in ancient Rome, Persia and Egypt. Most Roman cities had large public lavatories that became social meeting places. By 315 AD there were 144 in Rome, and people would gather to chat and gossip, much like in the public baths. For cleanliness they would use a communal 'sponge on a stick' which would be cleaned after each use in a moving stream of water in a gutter by their feet. Hence the unfortunate terminology 'getting the wrong end of the stick'.

After the Roman Empire fell, the sophisticated drainage systems were less widely used. The rough and ready Saxons and their counterparts generally used basic pots or shat in holes in the ground.

In the Middle Ages, the aristocracy demanded more sophisticated ablutions. The most advanced recorded was that of John the Fearless (1409–1413), the de facto King of France. His lavatory was attached to a 25-metre shaft that descended to the bottom of his palace where a stone septic tank collected his waste. It also had a padded seat and a heating and cooling system. John also had the pleasure of using cotton and linen as an early forerunner to lavatory paper.

In Norman and Tudor times, the populace did not enjoy much luxury. Some homes simply had holes in the wall to crap onto the street. The slightly richer may have had a small room extension sticking out of the side of the house with a hole in the wooden floor (still crapping in the street though). Most commonly, the contents of chamber pots would be thrown out of the window in the hope of eventually finding an open drain. Needless to say, the streets were not pleasant.

King Louis XIII (1601–1643) allegedly had a commode built under his throne that he would happily use while receiving visitors. Perversely, he preferred to eat undisturbed.

Henry VIII had a luxury padded lavatory covered with silk ribbons and gold fittings which emptied into a water tank rather than a pit. It was called a 'stool of easement', hence the wordage 'stool'. A high-ranking, but probably not very coveted, job in Henry's Court was the 'groom of the stool'. This official cleaner of the royal rear was employed to wipe his arse, sometimes, in lieu of any decent parchment, leaf or sponge, with his bare hand!

The courtiers and guests at Hampton Court would share the 'Great House of Easement' that contained 28 seats. These led to drains lined with brick which would wash into the Thames. These drains would be cleaned by 'gong scourers', young boys small enough to fit down them!

# LAVATORY ETIQUETTE QUIZ

This quiz is taken from the excellent website for the renowned World Toilet Organization, and compiled by Expert Rating

**1.** A man enters the Gents and finds one other man at the long bank of urinals. The other man is using the first urinal near the door. Which urinal should the new customer choose?
a. ○ The one furthest from the door
b. ○ One at least 3-4 away from the first man
c. ○ One within 3-4 urinals of the first man
d. ○ The one smack in the middle of the bank of urinals

**2.** What if a man enters the Gents and finds that every other urinal is in use (ie: the first, the third, the fifth)… which urinal should he choose then?
a. ○ The one nearest the smallest man in the room
b. ○ Any urinal, since they are all equal distance apart at this point
c. ○ None of them; the man should fix himself in the mirror until someone leaves, or leave and return later when there are fewer people in the restroom
d. ○ The free urinal furthest from the door

**3.** Women like to socialise in the Ladies. In what part of the restroom is it inappropriate to casually chat?
a. ○ Over the lavatory doors
b. ○ At the sinks
c. ○ While waiting in line
d. ○ While primping in front of the mirrors

**4.** Even if there are partitions between a group of urinals, standard urinal rules still apply, meaning don't use one next to someone else.
a. ○ True    b. ○ False

**5.** When is it appropriate to begin a conversation with a fellow urinal user?
a. ○ When you need to say something important to the other person, especially if in a business setting
b. ○ When you have some comment to make about the lavatory
c. ○ When the other person speaks to you first
d. ○ Never

**6.** What is the proper protocol for flushing a toilet?
a. ○ Flush once, make sure no second flush is necessary
b. ○ Flush twice, always
c. ○ Flush before using the toilet, then flush after
d. ○ Flush before using the toilet, then flush twice after

**7.** Let's say there are three stalls in the Ladies and all are empty. Which one should you use?
a. ○ The first   b. ○ The middle
c. ○ The last   d. ○ Any of them

**8.** Many people use a paper towel to open the door of a public lavatory after washing their hands to prevent picking up new germs from the door. But experts say that, in fact, there is something else in the bathroom with more germs. What is it?
a. ○ The toilet handle
b. ○ The handle on the bathroom stall door
c. ○ The sink tap
d. ○ The toilet-paper dispenser

Quiz Answers: 1.a, 2.c, 3.a, 4.a, 5.d, 6.b, 7.b, 8.c. These answers are not necessarily endorsed by the authors.

The World Toilet Organization also encourages the enthusiast with some inspired computer games. Go to www.worldtoilet.org and click on the Toilet Entertainment banner. We particularly enjoyed Catch A Shit (pictured to the left), Toilet Splash is another favourite for the whole family

# and the joys of THE LAVATORY

## BY OSCAR AND ANTHONY PYE-JEARY

## The World's Greatest Lavatory
### THE MAGNIFICENT TOTO NEOREST 600

The inspired precision-engineered functions available in this hi-tech masterpiece make it the most advanced lavatory in the world today.

1. The lid automatically opens as you approach, then closes and automatically flushes as you walk away.

2. The remote-controlled adjustable seat warms using variable temperature settings.

3. The revolutionary multi-sequential cyclone-siphon jet flushing system delivers higher levels of performance than you have ever experienced.

4. An automatic washing and cleansing system that provides a gentle front and back aerated warm water spray, which can be regulated for preferred water pressure and temperature.

5. It also has an automatic warm air dryer, and automatic power catalytic air purifier and deodorizer and an optional oscillating spray massage.

6. All remote-controlled with a wireless LCD panel, plus a discreet yet accessible manual overdrive.

Sir John Harrington invented the first semi-automatic flush lavatory for his godmother, Queen Elizabeth I, in 1596. She refused to use it, though, because she complained it made too much noise.

Alexander Cummings, a watchmaker, invented a much more sophisticated flush lavatory in 1775. His revelatory idea was to retain some water in the bowl after the flush so that it blocked sewer gases wafting up the pipes.

In the 19th century the population in Britain increased dramatically, and with no adequate sewerage system more and more waste was going into the cesspits. A survey in the 1840s estimated 200,000 cesspits in London alone. The drains overflowed before they could reach the Thames, and before anyone realised the dangers of water-carried disease, tens of thousands of Londoners died of cholera. In 1858, as a result of an unusually hot summer, the smell became so bad that work stopped in the House of Commons and plans were made to evacuate as far afield as Oxford. It became known as 'The Year of the Big Stink.'

When Joseph Bazelgette, the Chief Engineer with the Metropolitan Board of Works, devised a scheme to carry water away from people's houses and from the Thames into the estuary, he laid the foundations for the London Sewerage System.

Subsequently, Thomas Crapper helped to popularise the lavatory due to a number of pioneering plumbing techniques and renowned good craftsmanship. He was given a Royal Warrant to King Edward VII to install 30 lavatories in Sandringham, and the modern lavatory as we know it today was born.

## THE BRISTOL STOOL CHART
**Developed by K.W. Heaton at the University of Bristol and first published in the _British Medical Journal_ in 1990**

| | |
|---|---|
| Type 1 | Separate hard lumps, like nuts (hard to pass) |
| Type 2 | Sausage-shaped but lumpy |
| Type 3 | Like a sausage but with cracks on its surface |
| Type 4 | Like a sausage or snake, smooth and soft |
| Type 5 | Soft blobs with clear-cut edges (passed easily) |
| Type 6 | Fluffy pieces with ragged edges, a mushy stool |
| Type 7 | _Use your imagination! You really don't want to see this illustration._ |

## SUPERMARKET FAVOURITES!

**PLOPP** — A delicious chocolate bar with a soft centre from Sweden

**My Fannie** — Toilet paper from Japan

**Coolpis** — A refreshing drink from Korea

**POO** — A tasty snack from Indonesia

## EVOLUTION
### AND THE FRENCH STILL HAVEN'T CRACKED IT! ↓

HOLE

FEET

## eighty per cent

80% of the human race lives in Asia. 80% of first pregnancies end in abortion. 80% of Botswana is covered by the Kalahari Desert. 80% of the soldiers in the Zimbabwean Army have AIDS. 80% of aircrashes happen within one kilometre of the airfield. 80% of Americans die in hospital. 80% of all the almonds in the world are grown in California. 80% of the world's oxygen is produced by plankton. 80% of tigers do not live long enough to reproduce. 80% of a bee's day is spent doing absolutely nothing. 80% of all the motor vehicles in Thailand are in Bangkok. 80% of top-flight Japanese students have regular sex with their mothers. 80% of the world's opals are produced in the town of Coober Pedy, Australia. 80% of the lead produced by Italy is mined in Sardinia. 80% of the world's population ingests caffeine every day. 80% of Scotch whisky is made for export. 80% of American women own a diamond ring. 80% of Bolivian children do not go to secondary school. 80% of Britons cannot name the English King executed by Parliament in 1649. An ear of corn is 80% water. The human brain is 80% water, more watery than blood.

## eighty thousand

West Bank terrorists are believed to possess more than 80,000 illegal weapons. There are more than 80,000 streets in London. About 80,000 Americans are injured by lawnmowers every year. About 80,000 Japanese were killed by the atom bomb attacks on Hiroshima and Nagasaki. More than 80,000 Nepalese refugees fled to India in 2006. The US has arrested over 80,000 terrorist suspects worldwide since 2001. The US government provides airlines with a list of 80,000 terrorist suspects. About 80,000 Assyrian Christians have fled Iraq since the fall of Baghdad in 2003. 80,000 US women every year undergo unnecessary hysterectomies. About 80,000 new weblogs are created every day. British parents drive their children 80,000 miles before they reach 17. About 80,000 people have died in the conflict in Darfur, Sudan, through violence, starvation and disease. 80,000 people in the US have contracted cancer as a result of nuclear testing.

# QI ELEGANCE

## A pot-pourri of style and how to acquire it

by Kathy Phillips
International Beauty Director, *Vogue Asia*

***I ALWAYS WEAR MY SWEATER BACK-TO-FRONT; IT IS SO MUCH MORE FLATTERING.***
**Diana Vreeland**

Diana Vreeland (1903–1989) was the doyenne of US fashion editors – the *Devil Wears Prada* of her day. In her youth, she danced with the Tiller Girls, sold lingerie to Wallis Simpson and played tennis with Gertrude Lawrence. She shared a masseur with Queen Mary and was taught to ride by Buffalo Bill. She was a friend of Coco Chanel, Evelyn Waugh, Cecil Beaton and Cole Porter. She discovered Andy Warhol. She and her banker husband insisted on having all their footwear made in Budapest 'where they make the best shoes'. They were made of Russian calf and polished by the butler with cream and rhinoceros horn. The butler also broke in all his master's new shoes for him until they were as 'soft as butter'. Mrs Vreeland was once in her office at *Vogue* when she heard a clacking noise and asked what it was. Told it was a woman's heels, she replied: 'Fire her. I will not tolerate such distraction.' It was said her own shoes never touched the pavement. She was Editor-in-Chief of *Vogue* until 1971, when she was herself fired.

Few women, perhaps, have gone to quite so much trouble to achieve style, but many have gone to more trouble than you might imagine.

*NEVER FEAR BEING VULGAR, JUST BORING, MIDDLE CLASS AND DULL.*
**Diana Vreeland**

## CLEOPATRA'S DEEP RED LIPSTICKS WERE MADE FROM FINELY CRUSHED CARMINE BEETLES MIXED WITH ANTS' EGGS

### *Body*

Tattoos – from a Tahitian word meaning 'to strike' – originated in ancient Nubia in the 4th century BC. To puncture the skin and inject dyes, tattooists originally used boars' tusks or the shards of sea turtle shells.

**According to the *Oxford English Dictionary*, the word 'corset' was first used in 1299, in an account of the wardrobe of the household of King Edward I.**

Elizabeth Arden launched her Eight Hour Cream in 1930. The apricot coloured balm was not just for her clients: she also used it to soothe the legs of her thoroughbred horses.

**The Miss Americas of the 1960s were five feet six inches tall and weighed a hundred and twenty pounds. Twenty years later they had gained two inches in height but remained at the same weight. The torch-bearing woman in the Columbia Pictures logo was slimmed down to look right in 1992.**

Butt Glue: American beauty contestants use this to keep their swimsuits from riding up during competition. Flying High Enterprises offer it as 'a gentle roll-on body adhesive available in a 2 oz bottle. Washes off with soap and water'. Price: $8.50 per bottle. 'Put an end to those mid-floor routine wedgies,' says the ad.

**Proportionally speaking, more people in the US die every year from liposuction operations than in car crashes.**

Breast implants are so yesterday. *Perfect 10*, the United States' newest porn magazine, guarantees the first silicone-free pornography, with models guaranteed to boast only the real thing.

### *Lips*

In the US today, 1,484 tubes of lipstick are sold every minute. Many women feel as designer Betsey Johnson does: 'If I were dying, I would be in the hospital wearing lipstick.'

### *Pink is the navy blue of India.*
#### Diana Vreeland

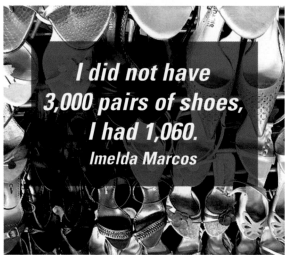

I did not have 3,000 pairs of shoes, I had 1,060.
Imelda Marcos

The word 'boudoir' was first used in English in 1781. Its literal meaning is 'a place to sulk in', from the French *bouder*, to pout or sulk.

Pots of red oxide of iron have been found inside ancient Sumerian and Egyptian tombs. Apparently lipstick is a timeless last request.

**Before collagen injections, women repeatedly puckered their lips with words beginning with 'p' to plump up their mouths. The early women's rights campaigner Elizabeth Cady Stanton (1815–1902) once said that she would not give any feminist literature to women with 'prunes and prisms expressions'.**

Despite this, in her 1963 *Beach Book*, the young Gloria Steinem admitted to sucking against the heel of her hand: 'This makes thin lips full, full lips firm, and fat cheeks lean.'

**Lipstick Pistol: Referred to as 'The Kiss of Death', the lipstick pistol was employed by female KGB operatives during the Cold War. The 4.5 mm single shot weapon was disguised as a tube of lipstick, easily hidden in a purse. For male Russian spies, an alternative was the KGB's single shot Rectal Pistol, which was encased in rubber and secreted where you might imagine.**

### *Hands*

Night Sky, a sparkling dark-blue nail varnish, was a best-seller for Chanel. One woman bought hundreds of bottles to paint her bathroom ceiling.

**Silkworm Cocoons: These are the latest thing in Japan. Known as *mayutama*, each one measures 3 x 2 cm and fits neatly onto the end of the fingertips. The sericin (silk) protein from the cocoon stimulates the epidermis and will naturally exfoliate and smooth your pores as you rub it over your face and hands. Order online.**

### *Face*

Makeup was an advanced art by the time of the ancient Egyptians. Both sexes shaved and pumiced their bodies and wore wigs, sometimes in combination with their own hair (a look later adopted by Andy Warhol). When archaeologists opened the tomb of King Tutankhamun they found a pot of 3,000-year-old makeup made from perfumed animal fat.

**The ancient Roman physician Galen (AD 129–216) is credited with the original recipe for cold cream. It was based on beeswax, olive oil and rose water. He also recommended finely ground garden snails as an effective moisturiser.**

Ancient Greeks wore false eyebrows made from dyed goats' hair, attached to the skin with natural gums and resins.

**High foreheads and the absence of eyebrows were made fashionable by Elizabeth I. During the reign of Charles I, children's brows were covered in walnut oil to decrease hair growth. Adults' eyebrows were shaved and replaced with fake ones made with mouse skin.**

Botulinum toxin (sometimes called 'sausage poison') is one of the most toxic naturally occurring substances in the world. Under the trade name Botox, it has been used since 1980 to smooth out lines and wrinkles on the face and neck.

### *There are no ugly women, only lazy ones.* Helena Rubinstein

Contrary to scaremongering, its history shows it to be profoundly safe. The minute doses used would need to be 60 times the size to cause any ill effects.

**The Korean Society of Plastic and Reconstructive Surgeons lists 1,300 members, almost twice as many as there are in California. Most of the world's rhinoplasty operations aim to reduce noses, but Koreans routinely have bridges put into their noses to give them more character. (Botox, on the other hand, is used to reduce big calf muscles, which cause Korean women psychological distress.)**

Women will do anything to conceal, bleach and blush. For two thousand years, European face makeup was made from white lead, which was combined with chalk or applied in a paste with vinegar and egg whites to mask completely the skin's surface and colour. The Spanish physician to Pope Julius III, Andreas de Laguna, complained that women's makeup was so thick he could 'cut off a curd of cheesecake from either of their cheeks'.

**In the Middle Ages in Britain, to fight the destructive effects of the lead paste on the face, noblewomen prepared their skin with ground asparagus roots and goats' milk. This was rubbed into the skin with pieces of warm bread. They used hair gel made from a mixture of swallow droppings and lizard tallow.**

As well as poisonous lead and mercury, women attached leeches to their bodies and swallowed arsenic wafers. To mimic skin translucency, the Greeks and Romans and, later, Queen Elizabeth I, painted the veins on their breasts and foreheads blue.

**Today, haemorrhoid cream is a well-known make-up artist's secret for de-puffing a model's eyes before a show. Preparation H is available from all good chemists for around £5.00.**

'Age Dropping' (starting plastic surgery in one's thirties rather than fifties) is the latest trend in America. The idea is never to age visibly at all.

*All the American women had purple noses and gray lips and their faces were chalk white from terrible powder. I recognized that the United States could be my life's work.* **Helena Rubinstein**

## Legs and Feet

Doctor fish are named for their ability to produce healthy results from even the most crusty or diseased skin. They are currently all the rage in spa treatments across Japan, China, Turkey and Europe. The idea is that you immerse your feet, hands or, if you're brave enough, your entire body in a warm pool that swarms with hundreds of hungry minnow-sized feeders. The fish zoom in on your flakiest, most scabby parts and chomp away at it to reveal the fresh layer beneath. According to enthusiasts, you emerge refreshed, buffed and glowing. Gara Rufa are toothless little fish originally from Turkey – they nibble but can't bite. They eat dead skin because they evolved in hot springs where very few plankton and other animals live, so they take what they can get.

**The Roman poet Ovid advised women, 'Let no rude goat find his way beneath your arms and let not your legs be rough with bristling hair.' Supermodels don't walk the runway with hairy legs.**

## Hair

The tallest recorded hair belonged to European aristocrats of the late 18th century, who stuffed their coiffure with wool or horsehair pads and kept it in place with wire, pomade and flour. Women had to crouch in carriages because their heads were too big to sit, and they had to sleep on their backs in order not to ruin the 'do'. In 1780, the doorway of St Paul's Cathedral had to be raised four feet to accommodate big-haired women.

**Dolls don't sell well unless the little girl can indulge in what toy manufacturers called 'hairplay', coiffing and combing the doll's hair. The makers of Barbie, the most popular doll of all time, produced a special 'totally hair' version in 1992: her hair reached to her toes. It became the best-selling Barbie ever.**

*Clive James described the torso of a body builder as a* **'condom filled with walnuts'.**

PHOTO: DONNA TROPE

COIFFURE A L'ÉCHELLE, CARICATURE DU XVIIIᵉ SIÈCLE

In ancient Rome, women bleached their hair using pigeon droppings. Blonde hair was considered to be the mark of a prostitute.

Of all 88 screen Tarzans, only one, Mike Henry, had a hairy chest.

**166 years after John Keats died, Dr Werner Baumgartner analysed a lock of his hair and found traces of the opiate laudanum. Each strand of hair has its own blood supply and reflects whatever is coursing through us. Drugs from aspirins to anticoagulants to thyroid medications can all affect the health of hair. Hair is such a sensitive indicator that drug companies are now experimenting with hair analysis rather than urine analysis.**

## *Perfume*

Assyrian men and women wore their hair elaborately braided, oiled and perfumed. Inside their hairdos, close to the scalp, they tucked tiny balls of scented wax. Melted by body heat, this trickled down the neck, allowing the wearer to remain fragrant throughout the evening.

*The Glove-makers' and Perfume-makers' Guilds were both founded in Grasse, Provence, in 1582. Perfume was closely linked to the development of glove-making. It was used to mask the unpleasant odour caused by tanning the leather.*

On the day before her desperate flight from Paris with King Louis XVI to escape the mob, Marie Antoinette hurried to Houbigant's store in Rue Faubourg St Honore to have her perfume bottle refilled.

**William Penhaligon, Queen Victoria's barber, created his first fragrance ('a subtle accord of jasmine and sandalwood') in 1872. He named it Hammam Bouquet, after the Turkish Baths near his shop in St James's, London.**

It takes one metric tonne of petals (8 million individual blooms) to obtain just over 2 lb of Jasmine de Grasse (the distillation of the flowers to make scent). To make 2 lb of the essential oil of roses you need five metric tons of flowers.

**One bottle of Chanel No. 5 is sold in airports every 9 minutes. There are nine ritual operations involved in sealing each bottle. One of these is *baudruchage*, in which a fine natural membrane is secured by cotton thread and knotted four times. This seals the top of the bottle to ensure that it's perfectly airtight. The term comes from French *baudruche*, slang for 'false optimism' or 'a windbag'.**

## *A little too stylish for my taste*

**Charlemagne owned eight hundred pairs of fine gloves. His excuse would have been that, at that time, gloves were difficult to produce and to clean.**

*The Duke and Duchess of Windsor had their lavatory paper hand cut, and footmen served their dogs from silver bowls.*

**The 2nd Duke of Westminster (1879–1953) had his shoe-laces ironed.**

*The singer, dancer and 1930s movie star Josephine Baker (1906–1975) used to take her pet cheetah to the cinema.*

**The New York socialite Rita de Acosta Lydig (1880–1929) owned eighty-seven identical black velvet coats that differed only in their lace trims.**

*The Italian shoemaker Salvatore Ferragamo once sold seventy pairs of his shoes to Greta Garbo in a single sitting, and a hundred pairs to the Maharani of Cooch Behar, who then sent him pearls and diamonds to adorn them.*

**The London residence of the designer Valentino has linen curtains that are taken down, washed, ironed and re-hung every day.**

## EUROPEAN LANGUAGES
### No. 5: French

**The French are sawed-off sissies who eat snails and slugs and cheese that smells like people's feet. Utter cowards who force their own children to drink wine, they gibber like baboons even when you try to speak to them in their own wimpy language.**
P. J. O'ROURKE

The average country French person has as much difficulty with irregular French verbs and with words agreeing with each other and with grave and acute accents as an English person does. Not only are most French people over the age of 50 unable to write grammatically – they cannot speak French properly either.

The circumflex accent (the little hat over a letter) represents an ancient missing 's'. It makes no difference to the way a word is spoken, so an attempt was made to abolish it by the Académie Française. This created such a storm of protest, particularly by those people who had one in their name, that the Académie was forced to reinstate it.

In 1880, a third of the population of London's Soho was French. British diplomats were trained by being sent there to learn the language.

The word 'etiquette' is French for 'label'. In French, a *brassière* is a baby's long-sleeved vest. A *chauffeur* in French means a stoker or fireman. Chauffeurs were originally French medieval bandits who drove their victims over hot coals.

There is no exact French translation of the English expression 'front door'.

### FRENCH DICTIONARY

**gland** acorn
**grappe** bunch
**prune** plum
**raisin** grape

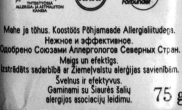

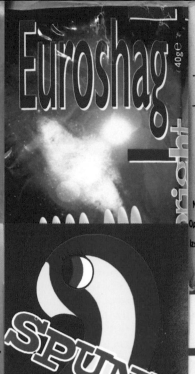

# EIGHTY-EIGHT USES FOR SAUSAGES

**According to the British Pig Executive, there are more than 400 named varieties of sausage in Britain, and an estimated 1,720 uses for them. We could only think of 88:**

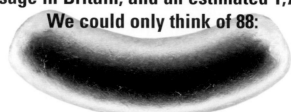

1. Pincushion.
2. Doorstop.
3. Paperweight.
4. Bottle stopper.
5. Low-maintenance pet.
6. Comical false moustache.
7. Novelty dog turd.
8. Faintly sinister buttonhole for Mafia wedding.
9. Biodegradable key fob.
10. Emergency cricket bails.
11. Aromatic candles for people who hate the smell of vanilla.
12. Stoat coshes.
13. German currency.
14. Speed bumps for model village.
15. Draught excluder for doll's house.
16. Show-jumping fences for mice.
17. Pick-up Stix for the short-sighted.
18. Butcher's bunting.
19. Relay batons for pre-school children.
20. Shoe trees for people with small, tubular feet.
21. Flush tester for lavatory factory.
22. Hair rollers for ladies whose husbands like them to smell of meat.
23. Handicap baseball bat for top player in game against toddlers.
24. Ten chipolatas will keep a pair of gloves shapely.
25. Nuclear submarine for fish tank.
26. Paint roller for creosoting shed.
27. Hand warmer.
28. Hamster bolster (place in baby's cotton sock).
29. Instant pork stuffing for roast snake.
30. Fingers for snowman.
31. Massive compensatory cock for Action Man.
32. Substitute torch batteries for torch that wasn't working anyway.
33. Flagpole for small, stout flag.
34. Pretend cigar for non-smoking movie mogul.
35. Voodoo doll for militant feminist.
36. Jiggle-it-yourself energy-saving vibrator.
37. Splint for broken finger.
38. Conversation piece for short, not very interesting conversation.
39. Device for distracting guard dog when breaking into stately home.
40. Horrible warning example to naughty pig.
41. Ornament which changes colour and texture over time.
42. Bookmark for one of those cardboard children's books with only four pages in.
43. Subbuteo flicker.
44. Ostentatious earplugs to impress upon others that you're not listening.
45. Sex doll for a slug.
46. Wind chimes for people who don't like the sound of wind chimes.
47. Window dressing for condom shop (if there is such a thing).
48. Scaled-down logs for foyer display of large timber merchant.
49. Incentive to dangle in front of carnivorous donkey.
50. Non-chicken drumsticks.
51. Replacement for lost lead-piping piece in game of Cluedo.
52. Easy-to-conceal truncheon for non-violent secret policeman.
53. Travel bathplug.
54. Rehearsal harmonica.
55. Edible perch for baby eagle.
56. Bait for dogfish.
57. Barrel cleaner for sawn-off shotgun.
58. Altogether more interesting *Big Brother* contestant.
59. Teether (exposes baby to salmonella, improves immune system).
60. Stylus for records you don't want to listen to any more.
61. Paint white and use as smart fenders for 1/72 scale yacht.
62. Pin two to an Alice band for instant rabbit costume.
63. Pin four to underpants for instant cow costume.
64. Glue parsley onto top to make realistic baobab tree for train set.
65. Use instead of air for puncture-proof inner tube for bike tyre.
66. Placebo in scientific tests of sausage-shaped drugs.
67. Retirement home for maggots.
68. Hands of unusual clock.
69. Tusks of unusual walrus sculpture.
70. Manlier alternative to liquorice in sherbet fountain.
71. Charisma implant for the discerning Speedo-wearer.
72. Necktie to distract attention from someone with weird neck.
73. Temporary stopcock for strange hole in wall of public toilet.
74. Hollow out and use as straw for milk.
75. Daub with ketchup, pretend to have amputated finger.
76. Now you too can practise circumcision without fear!
77. Ian Hislop action figure.
78. Something to produce when asked if you have a Nectar card.
79. Darts you can use in complete confidence that no one will die.
80. Stick several up bottom and tell doctor you think you might have haemorrhoids.
81. Eye-catching alternative to tinsel.
82. Edible solution to runny noses.
83. Crime-proof jemmy for burglars.
84. Non-vegan Rawlplugs.
85. Banana boat for frogs.
86. A common enemy for Israelis and Palestinians.
87. Leatherette-look gear stick.

88. Can be eaten with mashed potato, baked beans and gravy.

# EGYPT

**WHEN WEALTH HAS COME, FOLLOW YOUR HEART,
WEALTH DOES NO GOOD IF ONE IS MISERABLE**
THE MAXIMS OF PTAH-HOTEP (C. 2,350 BC)

THE EGYPTIAN NAME FOR EGYPT IS MISR, WHICH MEANS 'THE COUNTRY'. IT IS THE WORLD'S OLDEST NATION, HAVING EXISTED CONTINUOUSLY FOR 5,000 YEARS. ❋ IT IS THE 30TH LARGEST COUNTRY IN THE WORLD, FOUR TIMES THE SIZE OF THE UK, HALF THE SIZE OF SAUDI ARABIA AND THE SAME SIZE AS NIGERIA. ❋ ITS 79 MILLION PEOPLE MAKE IT THE MOST POPULOUS COUNTRY IN THE ARAB WORLD AND THE SECOND MOST POPULOUS COUNTRY IN AFRICA AFTER NIGERIA. ❋ IT IS ALSO THE WORLD'S DRIEST NATION, WITH LESS THAN A QUARTER OF AN INCH OF RAIN EACH YEAR. ❋ BECAUSE 90% OF THE COUNTRY IS DESERT, THE POPULATION DENSITY IS NOT HIGH OVERALL (IT'S THREE TIMES LOWER THAN THE UK'S) BUT ALMOST EVERYONE LIVES ALONG THE BANKS OF THE NILE AND A QUARTER OF THEM IN CAIRO, WHICH IS AFRICA'S SECOND MOST CROWDED CITY AFTER LAGOS. ❋ 98% OF THE POPULATION IS EGYPTIAN, 80% ARE MUSLIM AND THE NATIONAL LANGUAGE IS ARABIC. ❋ THIS IS QUITE SURPRISING GIVEN ITS SUCCESSIVE WAVES OF INVASIONS, NOT JUST BY MUSLIM ARABS BUT ALSO BY LIBYANS, NUBIANS, ASSYRIANS, PERSIANS (TWICE), GREEKS, ROMANS, BYZANTINE ROMANS, OTTOMAN TURKS AND NAPOLEONIC FRENCH. ❋ THE WORD 'EGYPT' COMES FROM AIGYPTOS, THE GREEK MISPRONUNCIATION OF THE ANCIENT EGYPTIAN NAME, HWT-KA-PTAH, 'THE HOUSE OF THE SOUL OF PTAH' (PTAH WAS AN EARLY EGYPTIAN GOD). ❋ 'COPTIC', THE NAME NOW USED FOR EGYPTIAN CHRISTIANS, WAS AN ARABIC MISPRONUNCIATION OF AIGYPTOS. ❋ BUT EGYPTIAN CIVILISATION HAD STARTED LONG BEFORE THESE CONFUSIONS: THE GREAT PYRAMID AT GIZA WAS COMPLETED 1,000 YEARS BEFORE STONEHENGE. ❋ IT TOOK 20 YEARS TO BUILD, USING A LABOUR FORCE OF 100,000 (ABOUT A TENTH OF THE WHOLE POPULATION) WORKING AN AVERAGE TEN-HOUR DAY. ❋ ALTHOUGH IT DEPENDED ON SLAVERY, THE WORKMEN WERE PAID — THE FIRST RECORDED PAYROLL IN HISTORY. ❋ THE GREAT PYRAMID WAS THE WORLD'S TALLEST BUILDING FOR 4,000 YEARS, ONLY OVERTAKEN BY LINCOLN CATHEDRAL IN AD 1300 ❋ OVER THE FOLLOWING 300 CENTURIES, AS WELL AS BUILDING OVER 100 MORE PYRAMIDS, THE EGYPTIANS — WITH A POPULATION NO LARGER THAN THAT OF MODERN BIRMINGHAM — INVENTED PAPER, INK, WRITING, METALWORKING, CONCRETE, WOODEN FURNITURE, BOATS WITH SAILS, WEIGHING SCALES, SHOES, CANDLES, TAPS, METAL SWORDS, CHARIOTS, MUSEUMS, SUNDIALS, THE 365-DAY YEAR, ALCHEMY, COSMETICS, PERFUME, FIBREGLASS AND A CONTRACEPTIVE MADE FROM CROCODILE DUNG AND HONEY. ❋ THEY ALSO INVENTED THE BUSINESS HANDSHAKE, THE WILL, MONOTHEISM, THE NOW UNIVERSAL MORAL PRECEPT 'DO AS YOU WOULD BE DONE BY', AND — WHILE MOST OF THE REST OF THE WORLD WAS STILL HUNTING AND GATHERING — THE WORLD'S FIRST GUIDE TO ETIQUETTE. ❋ THEY ALSO HAD THE WORLD'S FIRST FEMALE RULER — MERITNIT IN 2950 BC. ❋ MODERN EGYPT'S INNOVATION RATE IS, INEVITABLY, SLOWER, BUT IT REMAINS THE ONLY ARAB COUNTRY WITH AN OPERA HOUSE.

**AN ONION OFFERED WITH LOVE IS WORTH A SHEEP.**
EGYPTIAN PROVERB

# EXECUTIONS

## BEHEADING

1535 – Severed heads were usually boiled in salt then stuck on poles where they would stay for months. The head of John Fisher – executed by Henry VIII – 'grew daily fresher & fresher', leading to cries that it was a miracle.

1541 – Margaret, Countess of Salisbury, a game old lady well over 80, was condemned to death by Henry VIII in place of her absentee cardinal son. She refused to kneel with her head on the block and was chased, screaming, round the scaffold. Eventually the executioner had to push her over and hack off her head as she wriggled on the ground.

1685 – Lord Monmouth, sentenced by the notorious Judge Jeffreys, was still alive after three hefty swings of the axe. The headsman had to finish off the job with a knife.

1747 – The last person to be beheaded in Britain was Lord Lovat, an 80-year-old Jacobite. There were so many spectators that the grandstand collapsed, killing 22. 'The more mischief, the better sport!' chortled the ancient rebel.

1792 – About 10,000 people were guillotined in France between 1792 and 1799. Contrary to popular belief, more than 80% of them were commoners. The guillotine was also popular with the Nazis who used it to execute over 20,000 people.

1905 – A Doctor Beaurieux attended the execution of a criminal called Languille and called on the newly severed head by name. Opening its eyes, it fixed him with a penetrating gaze and was conscious for 30 seconds after the blade fell.

1977 – The last execution by guillotine took place in Marseilles, more than eight years after men first landed on the moon.

## BOILING & BAKING

570 BC – The sculptor Perillus of Athens designed a life-size hollow bronze bull for the Sicilian despot Phalaris. The condemned man was to be placed inside and a fire lit beneath, so that his screams came out of the bull's mouth. To test the device, Perillus was selected as the first victim.

1531 – Richard Roose, the Bishop of Rochester's cook, was convicted of poisoning 17 people and killing two. A special Act of Parliament was passed to allow him to be boiled to death in his own pot.

# SUDDEN EXITS & STICKY ENDS

1542 – Margaret Davy, a maidservant, was boiled to death for poisoning at Smithfield. The Act was repealed in 1547.

1603 – The Japanese Shogun Tokugawa Ieyasu boiled stubborn Christians in the hot springs of his favourite volcano.

## BURNING

1000 BC – The Druids piled living people into a wooden cage in the form of a vast Wicker Man and then set it alight.

64 AD – The Emperor Nero burned Christians as human torches to light the garden at his palace The Golden House.

1314 – When Jacques de Molay, the last Grand Master of the Knights Templar, was burnt at the stake, he swore from his funeral pyre that his accusers - King Philippe le Bel and Pope Clement V - would be judged by God before the year was over. They were both dead within eight months.

1535 – The tongue of Antoine Poile, a Huguenot condemned for blasphemy, was nailed to his cheek before he was burnt.

1553 – Bloody Queen Mary ascended the throne. In the five years of her reign she burned 300 people at the stake.

## HANGING, DRAWING & QUARTERING

1283 – The victim was hanged until semi-conscious then cut down and stripped naked. His innards were pulled out through a slit in his stomach and burned in front of him, after which he was cut into four with an axe. His genitals were often cut off and stuffed into his mouth. The first to suffer this fate was Dafydd, Prince of Wales, condemned for treason by Edward I. Women were never hanged, drawn and quartered because it involved nudity. They were politely burned to death instead.

1870 – Hanging, drawing and quartering was abolished in 1870, though, since 1814, drawing and quartering had been carried out posthumously.

Hanged bodies were known as Gallows Apples.

# Escoffier v. Mitchell

Georges Auguste Escoffier (1846–1935) was not only a legendary chef, he also existed and, to this day, is probably the most famous chef who's dead, and is likely to remain so until Delia dies.

## Above all, keep it simple.
AUGUSTE ESCOFFIER

*'Food, glorious food, nothing quite like it for cooling the blood' is a mixture of two well-known songs and reflects the views of neither.*
DAVID MITCHELL

### ESCOFFIER DOSSIER

Escoffier was the world's longest-serving chef: he worked professionally for 62 years.

He was the first great chef to work for the public. Before him, master chefs worked exclusively for the aristocracy.

He was the first chef to be awarded the Légion d'Honneur. He was very short and had to wear built up shoes to reach the stove.

His wife was called Delphine Daffis. They were married for 55 years. He died aged 89, a few days after she did.

But what did Escoffier actually do that was so great? Well, among others, these things:

He pioneered the 'brigade system' for running kitchens (which replaced the previous 'help yourself to whatever's in the fridge' system, which was a bit of a mean system until the fridge was invented).

He created the two most famous Melba foods (Peach and Toast).

He introduced 'service à la russe' to France, where, perhaps understandably, 'service à la française' had previously prevailed. (The difference between these services being that, in the old French one, all the dishes came all at once and sat there getting cold like bloody tapas, whereas in the 'à la russe' system things arrived course by course, as is now normal). And he basically made it okay and even a bit cool to be a chef.

A really terrific cook, then, he was also an astute businessman who co-founded (with César Ritz) some of the most famous hotels in the world.

Many would say he dedicated his whole life to food lovers.

I would not say that.

I would say that we should not mistake gourmets for food lovers. Gourmets are just fussy eaters – they have no love for food in its purest form: as it is found in a newsagent's. I, on the other hand, count myself a genuine foodie because, when I'm hungry, I find almost anything delicious.

No one who has lost touch with the deliciousness of a Scotch egg and a packet of Quavers, or a mouthful of shrink-wrapped ham followed by a KitKat can call themselves a genuine food lover.

Escoffier famously said of cookery, 'Above all, keep it simple.' Clearly he did not mean this. It's just the same twinkly dishonesty as when Gary Rhodes claims to be demonstrating a good old-fashioned fry-up breakfast and then advocates making your own baked beans. 'Keep it simple'?!? Escoffier invented 10,000 recipes! I don't think I've eaten 10,000 different things in my life. I say, 'Have a cheese sandwich for lunch every day for a month' – that's keeping it simple. Only a real food lover could get through that.

So I propose to take him on: gourmet versus food lover, master chef versus trencherman, Le Creuset versus Uncle Ben's.

## There are two things I like stiff, and one of them's jelly.
DAME NELLIE MELBA

## *Round One: Starter*

*Escoffier* (left) *vous propose 'Nymphes à L'Aurore' or 'Nymphs in the Dawn'. This was a dish created for the Prince of Wales and is actually 'lukewarm frogs' legs in a white wine and fish sauce with paprika, garnished with chervil and tarragon and served in champagne jelly'. He said it was 'nymphs' to make it sound more palatable to the prince, who presumably thought eating a river-dwelling mythical maiden was absolutely the kind of thing he should be doing more of.*

*My starter* (right) *is also served lukewarm: 'Crisps That Have Been in the Car'. I was going to go for something more complex but there's been a massive run on chervil at my local Londis. Nevertheless, I'm not stinting on service as I'm putting them in a bowl. Sophisticates may like to accompany their crisps with a tub of red goo – which you can usually find by the tills of any good video rental shop.*

## *Round Two: Main Course*

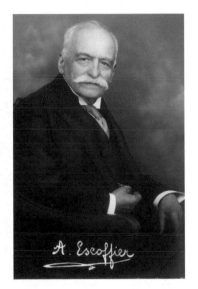

*Escoffier* (left) *vous propose 'Tournedos Rossini'. This is actually made of beef, not the famous composer, but there is no record of whether this made it sound more or less delicious to royalty. Some anecdotes claim that it was actually invented by Antoine Carême, an earlier French chef.*

*My creation* (right) *for the main course has also been attributed by the envious to other chefs: 'Chicken Korma with Pilau Rice'. Ingredients: 1 Packet of Chicken Korma with Pilau Rice (feeds one). Certainly there have been dishes of this name in the past, but my breakthrough was to see the advantages of limiting my cuisine to foods that already have cooking instructions printed on the outside. Not only is this convenient but it also guarantees that gratifyingly delicious amounts of salt and sugar will already have been added at the factory stage. Eat that, Escoffier! (He'd probably rather not, he's fussy.)*

## *Round Three: Pudding*

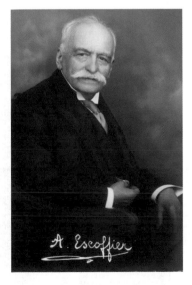

*Escoffier* (left) *vous propose 'Peach Melba'. Again dedicated to a muso, this time the opera singer Dame Nellie Melba, it's a sort of ice-cream sundae with peaches and, for some reason, raspberry sauce. I would have thought that kind of chocolate sauce that goes hard on the ice cream forming a sort of negative Alp effect would have been a lot better.*

*My offering* (right) *is 'There Isn't Any Pudding – Shall We Go to the Pub?' I must say my guests always find this very popular, particularly in the summer months when the smell of my kitchen bin can be a little bit ripe for some Korma-stuffed stomachs. And I find that two or three pints of strong lager really can perform digestive miracles.*

And who is the winner, Mitchell or Escoffier? You must be the judge. Just ask yourself which of the above menus you've eaten most from in your life, and give that chef a hundred points.

# The EGGHEAD ADVENTURES of THOMAS EDISON

Eggheaded inventor Thomas Alva Edison (1847-1931) was an extraordinary character. The true story of this oddball American's crazy capers makes comic book reading.

Young Thomas Edison was a prodigious reader, encouraged by his father, who paid him for every book he read. When he wasn't reading, Thomas would carry out scientific experiments. One of his earliest experiments was sitting on a bird's egg to see whether it would hatch.

It didn't.

COME ON! ONE MORE MOUTHFUL AND WE'LL HAVE LIFT OFF!

PARP!

SQUELCH!

OH CRUMBS! I THINK I'VE FOLLOWED THROUGH!

In another childhood experiment Edison induced a friend to swallow a large quantity of Seidlitz powders - a laxative containing tartaric acid, sodium bicarbonate and potassium sodium tartrate - in the hope that the gas generated would enable his unfortunate pal to fly.

Thomas Edison's schooldays lasted all of three months. That was as much as his teacher could bear. Edison is thought to have suffered from Attention Deficit Disorder, but his schoolmaster had another name for it...

AND DON'T COME BACK, YOU ADDLED RETARD!

OOPS! BETTER MAKE MYSELF SCARCE!

TAKE THAT!!

Thomas was almost totally deaf, and he blamed this on an assault he suffered at the hands of an irate railway guard whose train he had accidentally ignited during an impromptu chemistry experiment.

As well as an egghead, Thomas was an entrepreneur. He earned money selling newspapers, confectionary and home-grown vegetables to train passengers.

WAR DECLARED! CONFEDERATES ATTACK FORT SUMTER...

APPLES, BANANAS! 2 CENTS A PAAHND!

CANDY, CHOC-ICES!

He saved up his profits and invested them in a second-hand printing press...

...and at the age of 14 he was producing his own newspaper, which he edited, printed and distributed, on board a train.

ROLL UP, ROLL UP! WEEKLY HERALD ON SALE HERE!

I DON'T BELIEVE IT!

GADZOOKS! HE'S PRODUCING THAT NEWSPAPER... FROM A TRAIN!

Edison built his own telegraph system using bottles, nails and stove-pipe wire. He tried to generate power for it by *rubbing a neighbour's cat* to create static electricity.

HISSSS!!

That didn't work, but the system did... until the day it was wrecked by a stray cow.

# 1,000 patents weren't enough - He just kept on inventing stuff!

Edison worked as a telegraph operator and was constantly coming up with new inventions. But he had no joy selling them. In 1869 he arrived in New York, penniless, and was offered a job repairing telegraph equipment.

His big breakthrough was the Universal Stock Ticker, a telegraphic printer used for communicating stock prices to New York brokers' offices.

Edison was hoping to sell the rights to this little invention for $3,000, but he didn't have the nerve to ask for such a large sum. Which was just as well...

He spent the proceeds setting up the world's first industrial research laboratory, at Menlo Park, New Jersey. It was the ultimate garden shed! Inside it, Edison beavered away day and night, aiming to come up with a new invention every week.

Edison employed a large team of scientists and engineers who worked alongside him, but his hard-working assistants didn't always get the credit, or rewards, that their work deserved.

He was such a frequent visitor to the US Patent Office, Edison received an annual invitation to their Christmas party.* He held 1,093 US patents in total, as well as many patents in England, France and Germany.

\* Joke

Edison is credited with inventing, among other things, the phonograph (record player), the quadruplex telegraph (an early form of broadband, sort of), the movie camera, the fluoroscope (X-ray) and, of course, the incandescent light bulb...

Edison was definitely the first man to execute an elephant in public using electricity. He accomplished this dubious feat in 1903. The victim was Topsy, a homicidal pachyderm from Coney Island circus. Edison hoped that by pumping 6,600 volts of alternating current through the hapless beast he could convince the public that his DC electricity supply system was safer than AC. Topsy died in vain, and the AC system, promoted by Edison's arch-rivals George Westinghouse and Nikola Tesla, won the day.

A big concrete tower topped by a giant glass bulb now stands on the site of Edison's Menlo Park laboratory, a fitting tribute to his inventive genius.

And Edison's name lives on, at least in the pubs of Devon and Cornwall, where a band *claiming* to be the original line-up of the sixties chart-toppers Edison Lighthouse (whose name was inspired by the concrete memorial) perform their one and only hit, 'Love grows where my Rosemary goes', to ever decreasing audiences.

# E-COMMERCE

www.qi.com/mugs

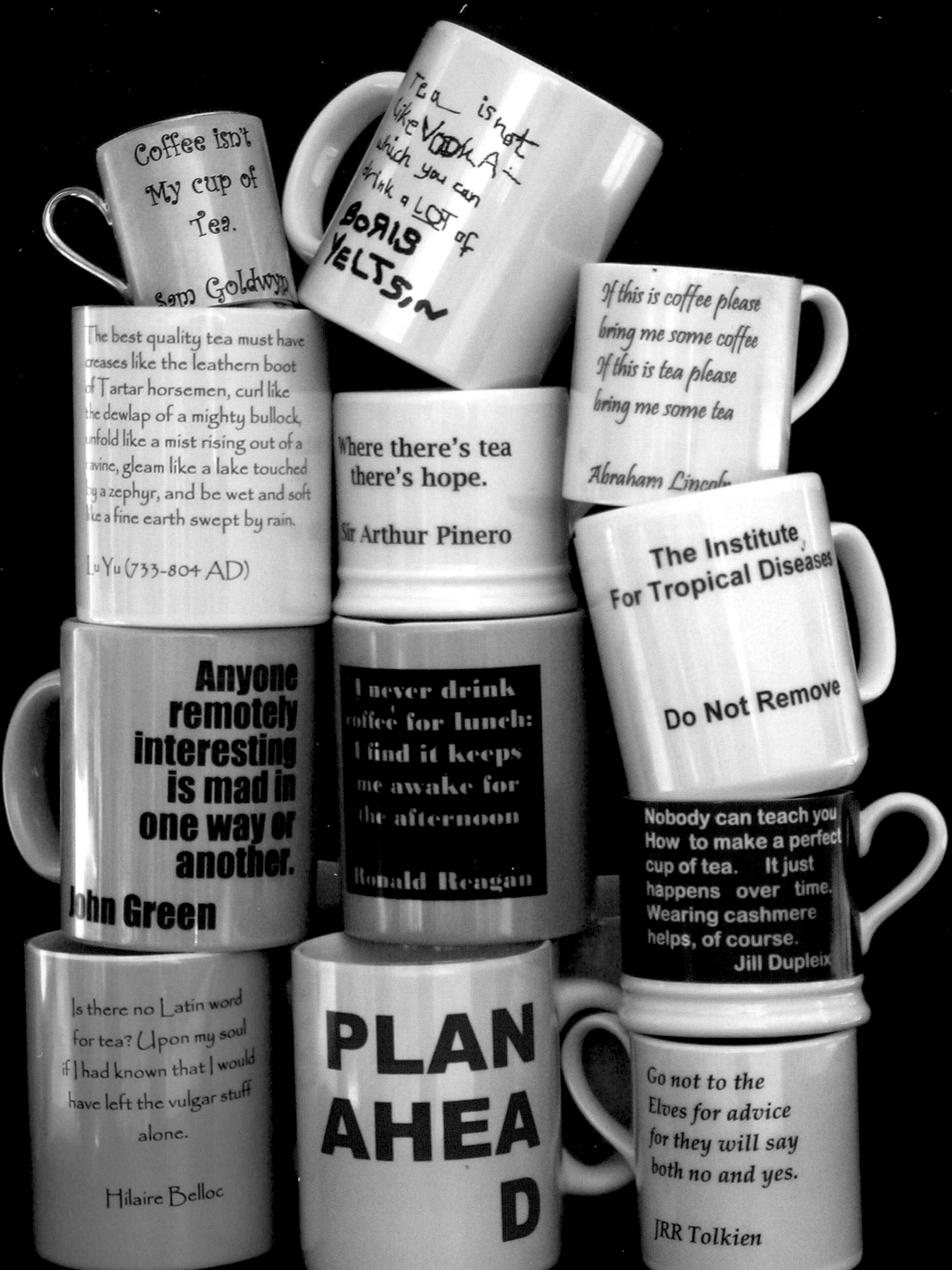

Coffee isn't My cup of Tea.
Sam Goldwyn
Tea is not like VODKA in which you can drink a LOT of
BORIS YELTSIN
If this is coffee please bring me some coffee If this is tea please bring me some tea
Abraham Lincoln
The best quality tea must have creases like the leathern boot of Tartar horsemen, curl like the dewlap of a mighty bullock, unfold like a mist rising out of a ravine, gleam like a lake touched by a zephyr, and be wet and soft like a fine earth swept by rain.
Lu Yu (733-804 AD)
Where there's tea there's hope.
Sir Arthur Pinero
The Institute For Tropical Diseases
Do Not Remove
Anyone remotely interesting is mad in one way or another.
John Green
I never drink coffee for lunch: I find it keeps me awake for the afternoon
Ronald Reagan
Nobody can teach you How to make a perfect cup of tea. It just happens over time. Wearing cashmere helps, of course.
Jill Dupleix
Is there no Latin word for tea? Upon my soul if I had known that I would have left the vulgar stuff alone.
Hilaire Belloc
PLAN AHEA D
Go not to the Elves for advice for they will say both no and yes.
JRR Tolkien

The QI Annual was written, researched, illustrated and otherwise enhanced by Garrick Alder, Ronnie Ancona, Clive Anderson, Rowan Atkinson, Pablo Bach, Bill Bailey, Jo Brand, Craig Brown, Rob Brydon, Jimmy Carr, Jeremy Clarkson, Julian Clary, Mat Coward, Alan Davies, Cherry Denman, Ted Dewan, Chris Donald, Jenny Doughty, Geoff Dunbar, Piers Fletcher, Stephen Fry,  Justin Gayner, Howard Goodall, Christopher Gray, Rich Hall, Martin Handford, James Harkin, Tony Husband, Phill Jupitus, Kate Kessling, Sean Lock, Roger Law, David Mitchell, John Mitchinson, Nick Newman, Dara O'Briain, Molly Oldfield, Kathy Phillips, Sandra Pond, Justin Pollard, Matt Pritchett, Anthony Pye-Jeary, Oscar Pye-Jeary, Vic Reeves, Arthur Smith, Mark Steel, Vitali Vitaliev and Tim Watts.

Edited by John Lloyd.

Designed by David Costa and Nadine Levy at Wherefore Art?
Cover illustration: David Stoten.

Project Manager: Victoria de Wolfe.

Picture research: Jon Petrie.
Etymological and Punctuational Adviser: Neil Titman.

Thanks to New Holland Publishing for the picture of the blowfly from *Nick Baker's Bug Book*, to NASA for the photography of the Earth and the Helix Nebula, and Donna Trope and *Vogue* (China) for the fashion photos in QI Elegance.

Respect and admiration to the anonymous geniuses of the qi.com forums, especially barbados, djgordy, dr.bob, Fudgie, grizzly, Mr Grue, Hans Mof, Neotenic, Not a Number, Peetay, samivel, Sebastian flyte, smiley_face, snophlake, strukkanurv, suze, Tas, Twopints, violetriga and 96aelw for thinking up 88 uses for sausages and for being generally good eggs.

Dedicated to Peter Ainsworth, Sophia Bergqvist, Christopher Broadbent, Jason Brooks, Richard Burridge, Simon Linnell, Ranjit Majumdar, Brendan May, Jill Parker, Lucy Parker, and Andrew Sunnucks – 'The Friends of QI' – who got the point before anyone else.

Photography: Chris Craymer, Harry Lloyd, Sarah McCarthy, Brian Ritchie, Dan Schreiber and Rebecca Waite.
Embroidery: Elizabethe Townsend.

QI Logo design: Jules Bailey.

With special thanks to Tony Cloke, Brett Croft, Olly Fetiveau, Mike Gornall, Brian Greenwood, Sarah Lloyd, Lise Mayer, Simon Papps and Jan Peter Werning.

*No animals were harmed during the making of this annual apart from the ones eaten by Jeremy Clarkson.*

*Additional photo credits:*
pp. 25, 30, 31, 48, 55, 56, 57, 65, 85, 88 *(Corbis)*
pp. 61, 85 *(Getty Images)*
pp. 12, 13 *(iStockphoto)*
pp. 17, 20, 33, 34, 35, 85, 92, 93 *(Mary Evans Picture Library)*
p. 54, final endpaper *(NASA)*
pp. 61,79 *(Rex Features)*
pp. 22 *(Topfoto)*

How inappropriate to call this planet Earth when clearly it is Ocean.
ARTHUR C. CLARKE

The Earth was small, light blue, and so touchingly alone, our home that must be defended like a holy relic. It was absolutely round. I believe I never knew what the word 'round' meant until I saw Earth from space.
ALEKSEI LEONOV, *USSR cosmonaut*

My experience helped me to see how isolated and fragile the Earth really is. It was also beautiful. It was the only object in the entire universe that was neither black nor white.
FRANK BORMAN, *US astronaut*

The world is but a school of inquiry.
MICHEL DE MONTAIGNE